GOD
IS FAITHFUL

DAVID DORPAT

CREATION
HOUSE
A STRANG COMPANY

GOD IS FAITHFUL by David M. Dorpat
Published by Creation House
A Strang Company
600 Rinehart Road
Lake Mary, Florida 32746
www.creationhouse.com

Unless otherwise noted, all Scripture quotations are from the Holy Bible, New International Version of the Bible. Copyright © 1973, 1978, 1984, International Bible Society. Used by permission.

Scripture quotations marked RSV are from the Revised Standard Version of the Bible. Copyright © 1946, 1952, 1971 by the Division of Christian Education of the National Council of the Churches of Christ in the USA. Used by permission.

Scripture quotations marked KJV are from the King James Version of the Bible.

Author's note: Some names have been changed to protect identities

Cover design by Marvin Eans

Library of Congress Control Number: 2007931875
International Standard Book Number: 978-1-59979-248-4

First Edition

08 09 10 11 — 9 8 7 6 5 4 3 2 1
Printed in the United States of America

CONTENTS

Chapter 1

A VOTERS MEETING, MORE DREADFUL THAN MOST

IT WAS FALL, and the church was packed for the voter's meeting. Its location was moved to the thousand-seat sanctuary because there wasn't going to be room for everyone in the basement fellowship hall. I was the reason for the crowd.

Over my then-fifteen years as a Lutheran pastor, as I visited with fellow clergy at conferences, pinochle games, family social times, and other gatherings, the meetings they most dreaded were the ones I most dreaded: voter's meetings. We Lutherans teach that believers are *simil justus et peccator*. That is Latin for "simultaneously saints [Justus] and sinners [peccator]." Well, the old *peccator*-ness of human nature really seems to come out at voter's meetings. Of all the voters meetings I had attended, I was dreading this one the most: the elders of the church were going to bring a resolution that I be asked to resign as pastor.

This voter's meeting was not just of local significance because this church, though in a small midwestern town (population five thousand), was denominationally powerful and strategic. Its membership of 2,500 was the largest of our denomination in the state. It included more than one hundred professors from the Lutheran College across the street. About thirty-five of them were seminary graduates, including many doctors of theology. The college was a school for the training of full-time, professional church workers. After graduation, virtually the whole enrollment of more than 1,700 would either go into the church's parochial school system as teachers or on to the seminary. Because ours was the only church of our denomination in town, these students worshiped with us. If a shot were to be fired at this voter's meeting, it would be heard around the whole church body.

To say the atmosphere was tense that evening would be a gross understatement. For months there had been talk about the prayer meetings that were being held in our home, attended mostly by students from the college. Every week from fifty to a hundred young people would pack our living room, den, hall, kitchen, and stairs. Bringing their guitars, tambourines, and other instruments, they would sing, worship, share from the Bible, and pray for one another. The meetings would start at eight o'clock in the evening, and sometimes the last student wouldn't go back to the dormitory until three o'clock in the morning. They were charismatic meetings in a time when the worldwide movement of spiritual renewal was in its early stages. Young products of the Jesus movement in California had arrived on campus the year before, along with students from other states who had been touched by the Spirit of God, and they came to our home meetings. The meetings were inspired, led, and empowered by the Holy Spirit. Miracles happened there. Young people who knew the Lord and wanted to serve Him came to deeply and profoundly love Him.

Their zeal spilled out onto the campus. Prayer and sharing the Word of God was suddenly happening in dormitories of a college that officially proclaimed Christ, but was filled with students that drank, partied, and lusted about equal to any secular school. Revival was taking place among the youth of a denomination that didn't believe in revival—a liturgical denomination that, as a whole, looked upon any kind of emotional, informal, spontaneous expression of worship with disdain. Spiritual gifts were flowing in a stream that was ice cold to them.

Don't get me wrong. I praise God for my denomination, the Lutheran Church—Missouri Synod (LCMS). It brought me the good news of Jesus Christ. It has resisted the call of modern theology's flight from the Scriptures. It boldly proclaims the Reformation principles of salvation by grace alone through faith in Jesus Christ alone, who can only be revealed through the divinely inspired Holy Scriptures. However, I believe the LCMS can and has at times taken on a pharisaic, sectarian spirit where everyone is expected to believe exactly the same and express their beliefs with the right words. For instance, in an attempt to protect doctrinal purity, fellowship with other Christians was frowned upon. Hymnbooks, prayer books, worship books, commentaries, etc. were only to be purchased from our own denomination's publishing house, lest our faith be tainted. These alone should be used in our services and organizations to prevent other thoughts or teachings from perverting the truth. When you feel you know and have all the truth, you're understandably closed to anything new or different, even if it's in the Bible.

I believe it was primarily the sincere and earnest conviction that the faith must, at all costs, be defended that precipitated this frightening (to me at least) voter's meeting. We will return to this meeting, but first, permit me to share some of the events that led up to it.

Chapter 2

I MET A PHARISEE
AND HE WAS ME

THE DICTIONARY DEFINES a pharisee as a self-righteous or sanctimonious person.[1] However, it was not always so. The Pharisees came into being as a movement in Israel during the four hundred years of history between the end of the Old Testament and the New Testament period, which began with the coming of Jesus Christ. It was a time when the nation was turning from God and His word. Israel was beginning to do what it had done so often in the past—hold hands with the pagan society around it.

There were, of course, strong believers who had not yet bowed their knees to Baal and who still believed in the covenant promises of God. A few of them, alarmed at what was happening, agreed that no matter who else would compromise the Word of God, they would not. While others might give in to the subtle, faith-robbing influences of the cults and culture around them, they would not give in. They would keep pure the Word of God and defend the faith. They called themselves *Pharisees*, the "set apart ones."

Their beginnings were godly. They were men and women of true devotion to the living God. But as time passed the original vision was clouded. They became prideful and preoccupied with their own righteousness, based on their conviction that they alone had the full, untarnished truth of God. They did, again, what Israel had done so often in the past. They became legalistic, making ends out of means. They focused so much on their manmade system of truth, which had been designed to lead them closer to God, that when God came and revealed Himself among them as a human being they became leaders in getting rid of Him.

I am a third-generation LCMS (Lutheran Church—Missouri Synod) pastor and proud of that fact. As a confessional movement within the universal church, the LCMS has held an important position of uncompromising loyalty to the Scriptures as the Word of God. While other main line denominations were giving in to the secular influences of our decaying Western culture, Missouri did not give in. As well as fallible humans could, we have kept pure the Word of God and defended the faith.

Nonetheless, the LCMS has not been exempt from struggles with legalism. We LCMS believers are zealots for righteousness by God's grace through faith in Jesus Christ. Considered the "the conservatives of the Conservatives", we have made ends out of means. We created faith systems on the belief that one is saved by pure doctrine rather than Jesus, the One to whom those doctrines are to lead us. It is as though we came to define *faith* as "believing all the facts about God to be true" (the demons know that—see James 2:19), instead of a trust in what those facts proclaim and give: a personal relationship with God through Jesus Christ. In the context of this kind of faith, true Christianity becomes little more than believing the right way and worshiping the right way, rather than walking humbly with God.

I still consider myself a Lutheran of the Lutherans, and I believe, as I always have, that the Christ-centered, Cross-centered, Bible-based Lutheran theology is the closest thing to doctrinal truth on this planet. I love the great Lutheran traditions, including the great Lutheran Chorales. True to my seminary training, I looked down on the subjective and overly emotional lyrics and melodies of the more contemporary songs and hymns. I remember in our liturgics class at the seminary how the professor mocked the music of other traditions by jazzing up hymns like "What a Friend We Have in Jesus" and "Jesus, Savior Pilot Me" and citing them as poor examples of hymnology. I laughed with the other seminarians, but I also felt uneasy about such ecclesiastical snobbery. As I look back on these things, I see that they were the marks of a kind of ungodly pride and legalism that permeated much of the LCMS at that time—two qualities that, sadly, seem to be making a strong comeback in our day.

Early in my ministry as I taught junior and adult catechetical classes, I was quick and thorough in pointing out the dangerous errors of the "heterodox" denominations. I thanked God that I was a Missouri Synod Lutheran and not like these other so-called believers.

During this time I don't remember ever emphasizing or even mentioning any of the areas of doctrine where we Lutherans agreed with the Methodists, Catholics, and other denominations. Far from it! In fact, I took every opportunity to point out our differences, virtually condemning them as heretics. I could go to another church to observe, but I would have had a hard time worshiping in such an "arena of false teaching."

In short, I had neither love nor feelings of unity or brotherhood for Christians who were not Missouri Synod Lutherans. This has been the heritage of a strong segment of the LCMS. I remember back when I was a student at Concordia Seminary in St. Louis, Missouri, Billy Graham was conducting a crusade in the city. He was at his prime, filling stadiums all over the world. Some students had talked to him and wondered if he would accept an invitation to come and visit the seminary. At that time our seminary was one of the largest in the USA and had a very good reputation. He was eager to come and visit, but when the students advised the seminary officials they refused to invite him because of our doctrinal differences.

I remember a sermon I gave in my first parish a little over a year out of seminary. The text was the first part of 1 Corinthians 12 on the gifts of the Holy Spirit. I was a subscriber to *The Concordia Pulpit*, a hardbound book of sermons for the whole year, published by Concordia Publishing House. In school students used to joke about pastors who relied heavily on that "blue Bible" they supposedly took into the pulpit, but during those early years I confess I often relied on this ready supply of material and, a few years later, even contributed a number of sermons to its pages. I was completely mystified concerning the nature of the catalogue of spiritual gifts in 1 Corinthians 12, so for this sermon I quoted directly from the *Concordia Pulpit*:

These gifts immediately fall into two categories in our minds, the gifts that no longer exist today and those that do. There are many questions about the gifts of healing, miracle working, tongues and their interpretation that should be cleared up. Permit me to comment briefly on these.

First of all they are now extinct and the fraudulent or perhaps well-meaning, but mistaken notions of some to make them gifts today are wrong [I then made the case against the gift of healing]. Another gift foreign to the church today is the gift of tongues which at times in sects has found its forgers. The tongues of the New Testament were foreign languages spoken by the person in an ecstatic state and interpretable by another person who knew that particular language. The tongues today are a lot of useless gibberish….the miracle-working gifts have ceased.

I was destined to gladly eat those words.

During this time I was quite authoritarian with the congregations I served. I was quick to correct people when in Bible classes, church meetings, or just daily conversation they didn't express themselves with theological accuracy or used words or concepts that were not "Lutheran."

In preparing and preaching sermons and teaching Bible classes, I had a niggling fear that I might say something that wasn't exactly in conformity with synodical positions or in synodical language. Pride, fear, intolerance, anger, antagonism, and insecurity—these were the marks of this doctrinally pure pharisee. Then something happened.

Chapter 3

THE REFORMATION OF
A LUTHERAN PHARISEE

IT WAS IN the fall of 1962 that my brother, Norm, and his wife, Donna, drove over from Washington State to our home in Coeur d'Alene, Idaho, to tell us about what happened to them on their way home from Moses Lake, Washington. They had gone there to hear Dennis Bennett, an Episcopal priest from Seattle who had been written up in both *Time* and *Newsweek* magazines concerning his experiences with the Holy Spirit.

As they were driving home from Moses Lake to Spokane they were talking about what they had heard, praying and praising God, when a sense of the presence of the Lord became so great in the car that they pulled off to the side of the road. There they were both filled with the Holy Spirit and began to speak praises to the Lord in other languages.

I was serving as pastor of Christ the King Lutheran Church in Coeur d'Alene, Idaho, and when they shared their experiences with my wife and me, I was not happy at all. After all, I was an orthodox, conservative, third generation pastor of the Missouri Synod, and those things were not done in our circles.

My wife, Donnie, on the other hand, was delighted. An adult convert during our courtship, she obviously had not been properly indoctrinated. She had recently attended a Bible class at our church on the book of Acts. She and another lady asked why the things that happened in Acts weren't happening today. The teacher said that "these unusual gifts of the Holy Spirit were for the apostolic age and not for today." I was that teacher.

Donnie pointed out to me and the class that the Bible says, "The promise is to you and your children and for all who are far off—for all whom the Lord our God will call" (Acts 2:39). She said, "We're far off and called, so why not us too?"

I don't remember how I responded to my trouble-maker wife, but I did notice that my brother and sister-in-law, who had always seemed to me to be two of the greatest Christians I knew, now were even more so since their experience at Moses Lake!

Because of what I saw in them and also at Donnie's urging, I borrowed my dad's Wollensak reel-to-reel tape recorder and went to Spokane to hear Dennis Bennett speak at a Full Gospel Business Men's Fellowship International dinner. He shared how the Lord Jesus had changed his life and ministry through the gifts and fullness of the Holy Spirit. I reluctantly had to admit that his theology was Christ-centered, biblical, and grace-filled (Lutheran, in other words). But I just didn't understand, yet, about this business of the baptism and gifts of the Holy Spirit.

Donnie stayed home with our four children, but I brought the tape home to her. She was listening to it while scrubbing the floor when she began to weep. She cried out to God, "I need this, Lord. Here I am an adult convert and pastor's wife. I can't even pray in public. How, Lord? How do I receive?"

Next month I went to hear a Lutheran pastor from Montana. Again I brought the tape home, and the pastor told her how. In those days tape-recorders were a clear mark of the Renewal. They were everywhere at every meeting. Just as the invention of the printing press helped spread the Reformation, tape recorders helped spread the Renewal.

As my wife listened, he said, "If you're hungry for the fullness of the Spirit, worship is the key. Go into your prayer closet and just worship and praise the Lord. You'll either end up going to sleep, reading a magazine, or you'll speak in tongues." It was evening. I was at a meeting and the children were asleep in bed. Donnie turned off the recorder, went into the bedroom, closed the door, and sang the doxology over and over. She didn't know any other way to praise the Lord. Sure enough, she began to praise God in another language. She also received a new freedom and boldness to pray and witness, as well as a great thirst to study the Word.

The pastor's advice might seem gimmicky to some. Not so. All God's gifts are received through faith. Worship and praise is the language of faith. It focuses upon the Source and removes doubt and distractions.

It took me almost three years of searching through the Bible, attending charismatic meetings and services, and countless people laying hands on me and praying for me before I was released.

One of the experiences that helped convince me to seek the fullness of the Spirit was a testimony we heard at my brother Norm's house. He and his wife Donna were leading a neighborhood Bible study/prayer meeting each week in their home and one evening Donnie and I joined them. To illustrate a point of scriptural truth, Norm asked one middle-aged lady to share a recent experience she'd had. This lady was a brand new Christian. She was biblically illiterate and had lots of questions. Although she knew that Jesus was the Son of God, that he had died for her, and that she was therefore forgiven and a child of God, she didn't understand fully about the blood of Christ. She said they sang lots of songs about the blood in her church, but she just didn't understand. One night as she was going to bed, she asked God to give her understanding. I don't remember if she said she had a dream or a vision—I'll call it a dream.

In her dream she began to hear a voice say again and again, "With exceeding joy... With exceeding joy." She said she had never heard such a deliriously happy voice. It bubbled with joy.

Then she saw the Lord. She didn't see his face, but she knew that it was the Lord. He was reaching out for her. As she saw Him, the voice went on and repeated again and again, "With exceeding joy to present you before the presence of His glory."

Then she saw, elevated and some distance behind the Lord, the throne of God blazing in such light that, although she knew God the Father was sitting on the throne, she couldn't see Him. She marveled that Jesus would be eager and filled with joy to present her to the Father!

Then the joyful voice went on, now repeating, "With exceeding joy to present you *faultless* before the presence of His glory."

She responded, "Faultless? You can't present me faultless. I'm such a sinner. I try not to, but I get angry with my children and nag my husband. You can't present me faultless!" Immediately the voice changed and became serious and said, "Do not trample underfoot the blood of Christ." From that moment she understood about the blood of Christ.

At the time I remember thinking to myself, "That is so Lutheran! We are justified and made holy, not by our righteousness or good deeds, but solely through the work of Jesus on the cross. It's only through the blood of Christ, like her dream said, that we are faultless. The devil hates the blood of Jesus. This *has* to be God!"

Norm went on to ask her to share what she had read in the Bible a few days after that experience. "Oh, yes," she said, as she opened her King James Bible (I guess it shouldn't surprise us that the Spirit knew what version she used) and found the place. "Just a few days later I was reading in Jude," she said, "and I came to verses 24 and 25. I had never read or heard this passage before, which says, 'To him that is able to keep you from falling and *to present you before his glorious presence without fault and with great joy—*to the only God our Savior, be glory, majesty, power and authority, through Jesus Christ our Lord, before all ages, now and forevermore. Amen'" (italics added). Her testimony took my breath away and set me up for what was to follow.

In October of 1965 we hosted Lutheran evangelist, Herb Mjorud, for a series of three evening meetings in a Coeur d'Alene junior high school second floor auditorium—an upper room, you might call it. At the end of each message Herb invited people to come forward to receive salvation in

Christ Jesus and/or the baptism of the Holy Spirit. The first two evenings, wild horses couldn't have dragged me forward. After all, I was the host pastor. On the third evening we had the Mjoruds and Norm and Donna over for dinner before the meeting. Afterwards we had a time of prayer and Donna saw a vision of three candles being lit.

That night in the auditorium, Herb talked about his aunt, who came over on the boat from Norway. She was a frugal woman and brought cheese and crackers along so she wouldn't have to go into the dining room for her meals. When some acquaintances she had made on the trip saw her on the deck eating her crackers, they inquired why she wasn't eating with the rest of the passengers. She told them of her dilemma and they responded, "Didn't you know that your meals are part of your ticket?"

Similarly, when we have Jesus, we have everything! All we need to do is by faith, appropriate what He has already given us—that is, walk into the dining room and receive. That night as Herb gave the invitation, this time I determined not to let anything prevent me from going forward. I was the first one out of my seat and the blessed Holy Spirit filled me. I spoke a few words in tongues, but the major manifestation for me was that I had such joy I could hardly stop laughing! In that meeting, leaders from three different churches received the fullness of the Spirit. Just as in Donna's vision, three candles were indeed lit.

I cannot remember a time when I did not know the Lord. Raised in a home where Jesus was known, adored, and called upon, I can remember seeing prayers answered in remarkable ways from childhood onward. In spite of this grace so lavishly given, I had become prideful and pharisaic. I can't say that I don't still wrestle with those failings and other sins, but I can say that since that night I was a changed person. I didn't have a great emotional experience. It was more of an absolute conviction that God was present and that His fullness and gifts were meant for me. The joy came because of that great knowledge. Since that time, God, through his Holy Spirit, has intervened in our lives with mighty miracles of healing and growth and has greatly blessed Donnie and me, our family, and our ministry.

One of the things I purposed to do shortly after that upper room experience was to write my classmates, relatives, and district and denominational church officials to share what happened to me. However, in spite of my great plans and fine intentions, the only letter I got off was to Omar Stuenkel, who had been my favorite professor when I attended Concordia high school and junior college in Portland, Oregon. I do not believe that was accidental. Rather, it was, in my mind, clearly providential. At the time, Dr. Stuenkel just happened to be on the staff at our publishing house in St. Louis. He published my full letter, withholding my name, in *Advance* magazine. As far as I know, it was the first positive article on the Charismatic Renewal in any official synodical publication. Following is the article, with my brother Norm's name changed to "John:"

> A few years ago John and his wife began to speak in tongues. There was an immediate uproar in the congregation. Eventually they were asked to leave the congregation. Reasons given boiled down to the fact that their conduct was not Lutheran.

If John and his wife had made a nuisance of themselves, it would be another matter. They didn't though. They didn't go around promoting "tongues." They did promote the Holy Spirit and faith in Christ. If someone would ask them, they would answer honestly, but they did not act unwisely.

All through this time my admiration for John and his wife increased immeasurably. They never once displayed any bitterness or hostility toward the members of the church. They spoke only of the joy and the power for witnessing that had come into their lives. Since that time they have grown immeasurably. They used to be my idea of the model Christian family. Now they are much more so. They are attending a small non-denominational church.

I have never seen people worship like these people. It is not unusual for them to stay in church praying and singing for three hours. And make no mistake about it, they give all the glory to the heavenly Father through Jesus Christ. They beautifully and consistently proclaim that salvation and sanctification is "alone by grace, by faith, through the Word." John and his wife regularly go down to skid row to witness to the transients there. Those they feel they can help they bring into their home. Someone is always living with them. They exude love and praise to God.

I have been studying this "Charismatic Renewal" now for over three years, listening to speakers, reading books, pamphlets, magazines, and, most of all, my Bible. I am fully convinced that this is God moving.

It is true that these gifts, as all God's gifts, can be abused as they were by the Corinthians. It is true that you can have the spiritual gifts and still be a pretty poor Christian. It is true that you can be filled with the Holy Spirit without the gifts. It is true that many who are filled with the Holy Spirit and manifest His gifts are also, in certain areas, in doctrinal error. However, none of these things change my conviction that God is moving today through the Charismatic Renewal and that if we oppose it, we are opposing God.

There are six main reasons that lead me to believe that this is of God:

1. The love that these "spirit-filled" people display for God and for people. I have never met more loving, self-giving people.

2. Their boldness to speak for Christ. They love to talk about Jesus.

3. The way they worship. They love to worship. Their worship doesn't stop in church. They are genuinely happy people who smile about Jesus all day long.

4. Their doctrinal purity concerning "grace alone, faith alone, scripture alone." They give all glory to God.

5. The Bible record. I have read books and articles against the Renewal too. And they gloss over pertinent Scripture like 1 Cor. 14:1, "Earnestly desire the spiritual gifts"; v. 4, "He who speaks in a tongue edifies himself"; v. 18, "I thank God that I speak in tongues more than you all"; v. 26, "What then, brethren? When you come together, each one has a hymn, a lesson, a revelation, a tongue, or an interpretation. Let all things be done for edification"; v. 39, "…do not forbid speaking in tongues."

6. My own experience. About three weeks ago, having added up all the above reasons, I felt that I couldn't put it off anymore no matter what might become of me. Although I was aware that almost without exception this was meeting violent opposition among Lutheran congregations I was convinced that this was God's will. So I said to God that I needed more of His Spirit, and if He saw fit to give me spiritual gifts, I was desirous of them, even that "lesser" gift, that "bugaboo" gift, the gift of tongues. And He gave. There was no emotion other than joy. I was in complete control of all my senses. As I thanked God I could hardly keep from chuckling out loud. In fact I did and have been ever since.

I cannot believe that this is all my imagination or that I have hypnotized myself or talked myself into something. I can't remember a time when I wasn't a Christian. I have always been happy in my faith. I have always loved my Lord from my heart. But now it's all "more so."

I would pray before, but now I can kneel at our altar rail at church by the hour and have the grandest time just praying and singing and being with God. After these times of prayer I am filled with joy, and I can honestly say that I love everyone. There is new boldness in my witnessing, new power in my preaching, new companionship in our marriage, new concern for people, new courage to be what I am in Christ.

Chapter 4

"I HOPE I HAVEN'T RUINED YOUR DAY"

A S A CARD-CARRYING pharisee who, as an LCMS pastor with a theology that was alone true, pure, and complete, my reaction to those who talked about encounters with God was to respond not only with great skepticism but with defensive feelings. While not necessarily spoken, my internal dialogue challenged, "Oh, so you think you have something I don't have? That's impossible. We have everything, and it's all in the objective Word of God! Subjective testimonies of God intervening in one's day-to-day life are suspect at best."

But now Donnie and I not only interpreted day-to-day experiences as gracious, divine interventions, we remembered past such encounters and began to praise God for them. One of these first such memories took place in St. Louis at the seminary after Donnie and I were married and had our first child, David. I came home in the evening after driving taxi on a slow day, having very little money and no food left in our trailer, except some instant baby oatmeal. "You can't have that. It's for Davie's breakfast," Donnie announced in response to my pained expressions. Then there came a knock

21

at the door. Our neighbor, whose husband was a medical student, asked if we could possibly use some spaghetti. "I made too much and Jerry hates leftovers," she said. We graciously agreed to help her out with her surplus. "Oh, I also made an extra apple pie. I hope you don't mind taking that too." We didn't mind. We really felt "lucky"!

There were also the many times that Mrs. Swanson, an elderly family friend from Minneapolis, sent loaves of her homemade Swedish rye bread. They always arrived when we were in need. More so-called luck!

We also recalled when Deanna was born in March of 1957, just two months before my graduation. Deaconess Hospital said I couldn't take Donnie and our new baby home until we paid our hospital bill of one hundred dollars, but we didn't have any insurance and we certainly didn't have one hundred dollars. When the day came to get her, I had just enough money for a baby sitter for David. I set out for the hospital anyway hoping that they were bluffing. On the way I just happened to pick up the mail, which consisted of two letters, one from Donnie's folks that contained a seventy-five dollar check, and one from my folks with a twenty-five dollar check! They had no knowledge of our need. You'd think I would have gotten the message then, but I didn't burst out with hallelujahs and praises to God like I would today. I just happily went to the hospital to get Donnie and Deanna and later wrote our folks about how "lucky" it was that their mail came in the nick of time.

On an early summer day years later in Coeur d'Alene, Idaho, I picked up the mail and found an envelope from a church in a small town in the Midwest. It held a letter from the senior pastor, who wrote that the previous evening the congregation had unanimously voted to call me as their assistant pastor and that the call documents would come under separate cover. In our denomination, the local church is autonomous and can "call," that is, seek to obtain, any pastor on the official roster of the Synod to come serve in their parish, no matter where he is serving at the time. It's up to the called pastor to accept or decline their invitation, still he ended his letter with the comment, "I hope I haven't ruined your day."

My day certainly was not ruined. It's always an encouragement to know someone wants you. However, both Donnie and I laughed at the idea that we would accept a call back to one of the hot, humid, bug-infested, flat, barren plains states, as we thought this one was. I don't remember exactly what I said to Donnie when I showed her the letter, but it was something like "over my dead body." We felt we wouldn't have to pray too much about this call. After all, we were home—just a forty-five minute drive from Spokane, Washington, where we both grew up. Both our families lived there. We had always prayed that we would be able to serve the Lord in the Northwest and were so thankful to be in a growing, active church in a beautiful town by one of the world's most beautiful lakes. Besides, now we had three more children: Deborah, Delisa, and Dayna. How could we take our five children away from their friends, cousins, and grandparents?

Donnie was the first to know that the Lord wanted us to go. She didn't tell me until I was sure. We prayed with Norm and Donna, with my dad, who was pastor of the big downtown church in Spokane, and, of course with one another.

I flew to Portland, Oregon, to meet with the senior pastor of the calling church, who was the chairman of Synod's Board for Higher Education. That board had oversight of the many LCMS colleges and seminaries. It was my first airplane flight and the propeller planes of those days flew at lower altitudes. Mount Rainier looked close enough to reach out and touch. It was a breathtakingly beautiful flight. "How could I leave 'God's country?" I thought.

The senior pastor was a wonderful man. I wanted to be sure and share with him my experience with the Holy Spirit, especially because of what had happened to Norm and Donna at their congregation on the north side of Spokane. Even though my brother was chairman of their congregation, Bible class teacher, occasional guest preacher, and he mimeographed the Sunday bulletin, their honest response when questioned about what happened to them at the meeting in Moses Lake was not met warmly. They had been so sure that the members of their small church—Christian friends they knew so well—would be overjoyed to hear about how God was working today as He did in the Bible, but the majority weren't. Norm and Donna had found themselves expelled from membership.

I didn't get that kind of a response from the dear brother from the Midwest when I told him about my stance on the Holy Spirit. He was gracious and accepting, seeing nothing in Scripture that would negate what had happened to me and agreeing that there was much to support it. My dad had suggested to me that if I took the call I might consider it wise to not be pushy, but to instead concentrate on preaching the gospel and following the biblical mandate to be ready to give an answer when asked about my personal testimony of the Spirit. I shared his advice with the senior pastor when we met in Portland, and he too felt that would be wise.

As I said, Donnie and I prayed a lot about the call, as did our friends. The more I prayed, the more I was convinced that, in spite of my arguments against going, God's will was that I should accept the call. Donnie then told me she had known that for quite some time. We got together with Norm and Donna and shared the news. During a time of worship and prayer, Donna shared a vision she had relating to our coming ministry in the new congregation of God reaching down, embracing me, and lifting me out of deep water. She also had a prophecy that we would have three years of wilderness and then a small, but rich harvest.

So, during the last part of August of that year we were off to the Midwest.

Chapter 5

THREE WILDERNESS YEARS

I DOUBT THAT THERE is another Lutheran congregation anything like the church we were now a part of. I am not going to mention the name of the church, the town, or any individuals. For the sake of the text, I'll call the church "St. Mark's Evangelical Lutheran Church" and the town "Centerville."

I have already mentioned that almost half the town's population of five thousand were members of this congregation and that because of the college across the street (at the time the largest of our Synod's institutions of higher learning) during the school year we had a worshiping community of over four thousand. I had no idea until I was there for a few years that it was such an influential church. And it shortly became more so. I think it was during our third year there that they moved the synodical district headquarters to this little town. Not long after, the president of the district and all the district staff became members of St. Mark's. If I had any ambitions for climbing the synodical political ladder, I was certainly at the right place. I would guess that there were more members of St. Mark's on official denomination boards and committees than any other congregation in the LCMS.

Centerville was a great town and a great church. It was an ideal place to raise children. They could ride their bikes all over town without fear of danger, and all five of our children attended the church's excellent parochial school free of charge. As far as we were concerned, it had the best teachers any school could get and plenty of young students assisting. Every school year, each of our younger children had a "special buddy," a college student who took interest in them, visited them in our home, treated them to ice cream at the college soda fountain, and took them on other fun outings, all as part of the student's course work. One call to a dormitory got us great babysitting. In fact, sometimes Donnie and I had to be away for a few days, and one of those times our sitter was the only young lady who was ever voted "Miss Congeniality" unanimously by her peers at the Miss America Pageant.

We were warmly welcomed to the church and community. The people were loving, caring and giving. For instance, some friends were visiting us from out of town and we were going to take them out for a little ride to show them around the area. As we were leaving our house they asked, "Don't you lock your doors?" I responded in jest, "No. No one in this town would steal anything from us. In fact, the only reason we would lock our doors is to keep people from bringing stuff in!"

When we got back from our little trip and walked into the kitchen, there, standing in the middle of the room, was a portable dishwasher with a note on it from a couple of married students who were going to be out of town for a while and were leaving it for our large family to use!

My title was assistant pastor, but I was treated more like an associate pastor. I shared the preaching equally with the senior pastor. In fact one Lenten season I was asked to preach for all of the midweek Lenten services. I was thrilled that attendance averaged almost two thousand each week. I helped in virtually every area of pastoral ministry in the congregation. My call also included working with the dean of the chapel at the college serving the college students. It was a challenging and rewarding ministry.

During our second summer after moving, we went back to Spokane for our vacation. While we were there, our sister-in-law, Donna, shared another vision with us. She described a house in detail and said she felt the Lord was saying that it would be a house of prayer. Donnie and I both realized that she was describing our home, but other than that we didn't know what she meant. We were and are a praying family, which, I am sure, is not that unique among committed believers. We felt that if this was from the Lord it had to mean more than that.

Donnie and I collected and reflected upon the prophetic words given to us about our ministry in this community:

1. We would have a three-year time of wilderness.

2. We then would experience a small, but rich harvest.

3. As shown in a vision, God was reaching down, embracing me, and lifting me out of deep water.

4. Another vision indicated that our house would be a house of prayer.

It would be difficult to call the first three years a wilderness when everyone was so kind to us. However, we did find ourselves struggling with the lack of Spirit-inspired, free worship; the lack of close fellowship and love that we had experienced in the Renewal; and with a serious family crisis, which I'll share in a later chapter.

The services at St. Mark's and the college were beautiful. Great, classic pipe organs triumphantly sounded forth, and professional musicians led. On special occasions, music professors and student music majors added other instruments that sent goose bumps up and down my back. The student choirs were of the quality that cut commercial records and toured overseas. They were all a blessing. The services and concerts were quite formal. Formality that expresses reverence toward God is fitting in the worship of the Almighty, but there are other forms and expressions of worship that are not irreverent and, I believe, even more biblical. For instance, there was no opportunity in town to worship the way the Psalms described, nor the way the New Testament taught and modeled. The many different Hebrew words for worship and praise in the Old Testament describe a worship that is spontaneous, demonstrative and celebrative. Clapping hands to the rhythm, loudly shouting praises to God, getting out in the aisle and dancing, standing up and clamorously raving and boasting about God, extending and lifting up hands, lying out prostrate in the sanctuary— all these very physical and emotionally charged actions are part of biblical worship. However, to do something even approaching anything like the expressions I have just described during the orderly, liturgical, prescribed worship of this congregation (and the vast majority of LCMS congregations to this day) would probably land you out on your ear and possibly get you committed.

Before leaving Coeur d'Alene, we had attended regular charismatic prayer and praise gatherings that blessed us greatly. In our new situation, we were able to travel to neighboring larger communities for Full Gospel Business Men's Fellowship International meetings and other such gatherings, but we did miss the more regular and intimate fellowship and worship we had known in the Northwest.

For us and other believers who have experienced the fullness of the Holy Spirit, freedom in corporate worship is vital, a fact that made the more rigid worship experiences at St. Mark's difficult for us. However, God is faithful and provided many marvelous worship encounters during those three years through which the Holy Spirit ministered to us and through us. The love, affection, and gracious embrace we received from the senior pastor and staff, the college community, and the townspeople was a clear extension of God's hand of provision over that need in our lives.

Chapter 6

JOHN CHAPTER SIX

ANOTHER PRAISEWORTHY ASPECT of this season in our lives was the shift in the focus of my ministry. The sixth chapter of John's Gospel turned on a light in my spirit concerning the meaning of faith. Any orthodox Lutheran should have a detailed understanding and ability to communicate two of the central elements of our theology: *sola fide* (alone by faith) and *sola gratia* (alone by grace). Otherwise stated, we are saved alone by God's grace through faith in Jesus Christ, His Son. These two phrases affect everything we teach. For St. Paul (and, we believe, all the rest of the New Testament Scripture writers) and Lutherans, the cross is the chief and foremost symbol of the Christian faith. In fact, our professor of homiletics (the study of how to preach) insisted that every sermon should include a presentation of the atoning work of Christ. Without it there is no power for salvation or, he said, for Christian living.

Yet I long had been troubled by the lack of the fruit of faith among Lutherans, including myself. I found firsthand that many students preparing for the preaching or teaching ministries in our preparatory high schools, junior colleges, teacher's colleges, and seminaries could drink, cuss, party, and lust on a par with some of the world's worst sinners. I remember how, in one of our LCMS pastor's circuit meetings in Idaho (monthly gatherings of LCMS clergy in a geographic locality, or circuit, for fellowship and professional growth), one of the brothers shared that one of his young students, after two years of confirmation instruction and just before Confirmation Sunday, approached him to explain that he had been at a youth retreat with a friend from another church and had gotten saved. The usual Lutheran response to such a statement would be to tell the young man that he had been saved when he was baptized as an infant, and if he had fallen away from that into unbelief, he surely would have been brought back through Christ in Sunday school and confirmation instruction. But this pastor didn't say these things. He believed the young man. He saw the change in his life and the sincerity of his confession of faith. As a young pastor, this boggled my mind. If it's one thing we make clear to our confirmation students, it's the gospel. And as Romans 1:16 says, the gospel is "the power of God for salvation." All we need to do is see that people know the gospel and the Spirit does the rest. That student, as well as the other kids and their families, heard that taught every Sunday without fail. How could they not be saved?

From that time on, I regularly tested the students with the following essay question to be sure they knew and understood the facts of the gospel: "You are driving your bike on a country road. A car speeds past you, spins out of control, and rolls over into the ditch. The driver is thrown out and badly hurt. He calls out to you, 'I am dying. How do I get to heaven?' Write down what you would tell him." If they said that they would tell the man that he could be saved by repenting and believing that Jesus, God's Son, came to earth to die on the cross so that the dying driver could be forgiven of his sins, I knew that the students must be saved.

Shortly thereafter, God opened my eyes to see that just knowing and believing the facts is not saving faith. He did it through chapter six of the Gospel of John. We were studying John in Bible class and I came to believe that chapter six is primarily a treatise on faith—faith that is not just belief in facts *about* God, His Son and the gospel, but a saving faith that is a personal, experiential, life-changing relationship with Jesus, wrought in the heart of the believer through the Word of God by the Holy Spirit. I was so excited about this discovery that I taught John 6 every opportunity I had. When we accepted the call to St. Mark's and moved to Centerville, I determined to not major on the Holy Spirit and His gifts (except when asked), but to instead be an instrument of the Spirit to bring everyone I could from belief in facts to a personal relationship with Jesus Christ. Every adult and junior confirmation class was taught that chapter. When asked to address a college class, if it was up to me, they got John 6. When speaking to women's groups, men's groups, youth groups, neighboring parishes, Sunday morning and home Bible classes, they all got John 6.

They were also asked, usually at the beginning of the session, this question: "Is it possible to believe all the truths of the gospel, that Jesus is the Son of God, that He lived, died, and rose from the dead so that you might be forgiven of your sins, and still not be saved?" Most everyone answered that question with a resounding, "No! If you know and believe those things, you are a believer. You are a Christian." I would then point out that the devil knows all those things to be true. He knows the gospel. I would then explain how John 6 provides a complete description of saving faith. I noticed that as I walked people through this great chapter from John, asking questions as we went, I invariably got the same wrong answers.

Allow me to share John 6 with you, using the Revised Standard Version:

John 6:1–14 begins with the story of the miraculous feeding of the five thousand. It tells about the miracle and how the people were so impressed that they wanted to make Jesus their king. (See verses 14–15.) What's so bad about that idea? Christ told Pilate that's why He was born into this world. What an opportunity! If only Jesus had had some kind of manager or public relations whiz on his staff, he could have really taken advantage of this popularity. He literally had them eating out of his hand, but He didn't even take an offering. Instead He completely dropped the ball and withdrew up to a mountain by Himself, leaving behind the chance of a lifetime.

When evening came, the disciples got into a boat and started across the Sea of Galilee toward Capernaum. In the midst of strong winds, they were frightened to see Jesus walking on the sea toward them, but He reassured them, "It is I, do not be afraid" (v. 20). They gladly took Him into the boat and suddenly they had arrived at the shores of Capernaum (v. 16–21).

The next day the throng of people on the other side of the lake saw that Jesus had gone up into the hills and that the disciples went across the sea, but they couldn't find Jesus. When some boats from Tiberias came along, they got on board and went to Capernaum to seek Jesus (v. 22–24). When the people found Him, they asked Him a logical question, "Rabbi, when did you come here?" (v. 25). Instead of answering their question, Jesus answered another question, why *they* were there and had followed Him.

At this point, I would ask the class I was teaching to answer that question—why were they looking for Jesus?—without looking at the text. Invariably I would receive some form of the answer, "They were following Jesus because they saw Him perform a miracle," implying that this was and is a bad reason to follow Jesus. I began to notice a very anti-miracle attitude among a lot of Lutherans, including, I later discovered, Lutheran theologians.

I would then have them read verse 26: "Jesus answered them, 'Truly, truly, I say to you, you seek me, not because you saw signs, but because you ate your fill of the loaves.'" Miracles are called *signs* in John's Gospel because they served (and still serve) the same function one of those old metal signs of an outstretched hand with its index finger pointing to a store, a doorway, or whatever. The miracles pointed to Jesus and say, "He's here. The King is here!"

Nonetheless, the people who followed Christ across the lake didn't get the message of the sign. The kingdom was at hand, but they weren't there to worship the King. All they wanted was what they could get out of Him.

So Jesus exhorted them to not "labor for the food which perishes, but for the food which endures to eternal life, which the Son of man will give to you" (v. 27). He told them that this food was a gift from the Father. It is "the bread of God...which comes down from heaven, and gives life to the world" (v. 33). Their response was an enthusiastic, "Give us this bread always" (vs. 34).

At this point I would again ask the class to tell me, without looking at the text, what they believe this bread from heaven is. Invariably I would get answers like salvation, forgiveness of sins, eternal life, peace, joy, etc. I then would ask someone to read verse 35: "Jesus said to them, 'I am the bread of life.'" It's Jesus we need, not what we can get out of Him.

He then went on to tell the crowd (vv. 35–40) that those who come to Him would have their hunger and thirst satisfied, that He would not cast them out, and that He came down from heaven to do the will of his Father who sent Him. He explained that the Father's will is that He lose none given to Him by the Father, but that all who see Him (Jesus) and believe in Him would have eternal life. Jesus also promised to raise them up at the last day.

The text doesn't say how many people Jesus was talking to. The day before, it was five thousand men plus women and children. It might have been a small group or a very large one that sought Him out and found Him. At any rate, as Jesus spoke a murmur began to rumble through the crowd (v. 42). "He came down from heaven? We knew him when he was a kid! We know his mom and dad."

In response to their murmurings, He just repeats what he said, except in more words, and then adds the clincher in verse 51: "I am the living bread which came down from heaven; if any one eats of this bread, he will live for ever; and the bread which I shall give for the life of the world is my flesh."

Well, you can imagine what happened next. Now it's not murmuring. It is loud disputation (v. 52): "How can this man give us his flesh to eat?"

As the gentle Shepherd, should He not gather them around to tell them winsomely, kindly, clearly, and simply what he is talking about? Well, look what Jesus does. He knows and obeys their Jewish dietary laws concerning what a person can and cannot eat and drink, including the directive to bleed all allowed animals (which of course did not include people) before consumption. No Jew could eat or drink any blood "for the life of the flesh is in the blood" (Lev. 17:11). Nonetheless, not once, not twice, but six times in six straight verses He tells them to eat His flesh and drink His blood (v. 53–58).

We are told that "After this many of his disciples drew back and no longer went about with him" (v. 66). He lost them! One day he had five thousand and the next He's back down to the twelve and asks them, "Do you also wish to go away?" (v. 67). I love Peter's answer, "Lord, to whom shall we go?" (v. 68). At first read, it may seem as if he is saying that they might consider leaving if there were someone else to follow, but then he makes his great confession: "You have the words of eternal life; and we have believed, and have come to know, that you are the Holy One of God" (v. 68–69).

Why doesn't Jesus make it simpler? Why does He seem to deliberately offend them, and what does He mean by,

"Eat my flesh and drink my blood"? Of course, as Lutherans who believe in the real presence of the Lord in the sacrament of Holy Communion, it is natural to suppose that that is the main thing he is talking about. But in the first of those six verses, He says "unless you eat of the flesh of the Son of man and drink His blood, you have no life in you" (v. 53). Even a child who believes in Jesus can have His life in him long before he ever goes to the Lord's Supper. That is not primarily what Jesus is talking about in this chapter. There's only one thing that prevents us from the life of God that is in Jesus Christ—unbelief. He's talking about faith!

To those who only want to be around Jesus because of what they can get out of Him, He is saying, "What you need is Me. Your primary need is not bread or forgiveness or salvation or joy or peace. All of these things you will find in Me." Faith is not just believing things *about* Jesus. It is laying hold of Jesus and taking Him into yourself by receiving Him into your heart and spirit. (See John 1:12). Faith must involve a personal relationship with the living God. The truth that sets us free does not consist primarily in facts, but in the reality of a living Savior and Lord whom we can know and experience personally. It is His life and presence that is the truth.

It wasn't until later that I remembered that one of the issues of the Reformation was just this issue of a "historical" faith, that is, belief in just historical facts about God versus true faith as described above. While in Centerville, I was delighted to discover these quotations from Martin Luther that assured me that I wasn't being "un-Lutheran" in all of this:

Thus Peter explains it, and correctly so: "Grow in the knowledge of our Lord Jesus Christ" (2 Peter 3:18)....This knowledge is faith itself, not only a historical faith, which the devil also has and with which he confesses God as the heretics do, too. It is rather a knowledge which rests on experience, and faith. This word "knowing" means as much as: "Adam knew his wife" (Gen. 4:1), that is, he "knew her by sense of feeling, he found her to be his wife, not in speculative or historical way but by experience.[1]

With extended arms true faith joyfully embraces the Son of God, who was given into death for it, and says: My beloved is mine, and I am His.[2]

I even found that Luther dealt with John chapter 6, in the same way I did. He calls faith "spiritual eating" in a December, 1530, sermon on John 6:32–35: "If you do not want to die or be damned, then come to Christ, believe on Him, hold to Him, eat this spiritual food. Let this be your primary concern."[3]

I'm convinced that it is possible that a denomination, a local congregation, and an individual believer can value and emphasize purity of doctrine in such a way and to such an extent that an atmosphere of ecclesiastical political correctness is established. When that happens, the ancient error of Israel arises. Means become ends. The Law, the temple, and the sacrificial system in the Old Testament were all means meant to lead the believer to a devoted worship and trust relationship with God. They were the means. The end, the goal, of those means was God Himself. Still, again and again Israel focused on and became devoted to the means, neglecting true repentance and trust in God. (See Jeremiah 7.)

I remember from my confirmation instruction as a boy, John 5:39 was used as a proof text to indicate the rightful centrality of the Word of God. It was often mentioned in sermons and counseling as a command: "Search the scriptures; for in them ye think ye have eternal life: and they are they which testify of me" (KJV). It's ironic that the main point was being missed in this so-called proof text! Just searching the Scriptures and believing them doesn't necessarily give life. It didn't to those whom Jesus was addressing!

A more modern translation says it like it is: "You diligently study the Scriptures because you think that by them you possess eternal life. These are the Scriptures that testify about me, yet you refuse to come to me to have life" (John 5:39–40).

The Word and sacraments are means, avenues to God. Their goal is that through them we might know, trust in, serve, grow in our relationship with, and love Almighty God. The multitudes of Lutherans who answered my question, What is this bread from heaven? by saying that salvation, forgiveness, and eternal life are the true bread from heaven were expressing the same attitude that the five thousand expressed. They wanted what they could get out of Jesus. They were making means into ends and vice versa. Jesus is not a means to a goal. He *is* the goal. It is to Jesus we must come. It is Him we need, and when we have Him we have everything.

> He who has the Son has life; he who does not have the Son of God does not have life.
>
> —1 John 5:12

Chapter 7

BUT, PASTOR,
IS IT LUTHERAN?

IN PREVIOUS CHAPTERS I mentioned my brother and
sister-in-law. They were the ones who brought Donnie
and me the news of the renewal in the Holy Spirit. As
I mentioned, they had been model Christians, but now they
were even more so. If I would have thought about it at the
time, I think I might have called them "New Testament
Christians" or "full of the Holy Spirit."

It wasn't long, however, that people began to talk. Some
had noticed a change in Norm and Donna and asked them
about it. They shared what happened to them and the word
soon got around the congregation. Sally Smith in particular
began to talk. She had always been very close to Donna
and, in fact, had called her almost daily on the phone and
talked for some time about various concerns. She had come
to lean on Donna as someone with whom she could share,
but now she apparently felt she couldn't continue their close
relationship. For some reason, Donna's experience seemed to
have become a threat and a barrier to her. She began to call
other members of the congregation and express her feelings.
In the end, Norm and Donna were called before a kind of

trial which consisted of a series of meetings involving the congregation and what our denomination calls the "circuit counselor"—a local pastor elected by his peers to council in such and other situations. At the time, my father happened to be the circuit counselor, but he excused himself. The district president appointed another man.

The final recommendations from these meetings indicated that Norm and Donna should either stop testifying about what had happened to them or leave the congregation. Simply put, the reason for this conclusion was that what they had claimed to experience was not Lutheran.

In examining the results of other such investigations and trials, particularly of pastors and teachers in the LCMS, I have discovered that no matter how many reasons are given for relieving the individual of his or her position, they all boil down to the statement that what happened to him or her is not denominationally acceptable. I've heard of similar results in other denominations, the only difference being, of course, that what was happening there was not Baptist, or not Episcopalian, or not Methodist, etc.

I can remember the question of the elders of two different congregations as I shared with them what happened to my wife and me: "Yes, pastor, but is it Lutheran?" That question is un-Lutheran! It's un-Lutheran because it sets Lutheran dogma and tradition above Scripture. A basic tenet of the Lutheran church (and lots of other denominations) is that the only source and norm of our Christian faith is the Holy Scriptures. In almost every case I have investigated, the Bible was studied at first, but was sooner or later dropped.

Denominational tradition and writings were appealed to and not Scripture.

As I saw this happen again and again to others and in my own experience, I began to see that the question was not merely un-Lutheran. Rather, it strikes at the core of our Christian faith because it can reveal a basic lack of faith in Jesus Christ and also lead to a refusal to listen to and believe His word. In other words, in Lutheran terms, the question, Is it Lutheran? can and often does proceed from a denial of *sola fide* (alone by faith) and *sola scriptura* (alone the Scriptures). To elaborate:

As I mentioned in the last chapter, one of the issues of the Reformation was the difference between "historical" faith and "saving" faith. Saving faith is a personal relationship with Jesus, while historical faith is simply knowledge of truths or understanding and acceptance of facts. Luther makes the distinction clear when he says:

> It should be noted that there are two ways of believing, in the first place, concerning God, that is, believing that what is said about God is true, just as I believe that what men say about the Turk, the devil and hell is true. This kind of faith is knowledge or information rather than faith. Secondly, there is faith in God. This faith is mine when I not only hold what is said about God to be true, but put my trust in Him, undertake to deal with Him personally.[4]

It has been my experience that the general mind-set reflected in the question, Is it Lutheran? is one which clings to historical faith as the means of salvation. This attitude says, "If I believe all the correct propositions, the doctrinal formulas, the truths, the objective facts about Jesus and about God and the way of salvation, I am saved." And, because the individual has come to know this information, these formulas, and facts through a denomination, they become identified with that denomination. The denomination then becomes his savior, and anything that is outside of this tradition is threatening because the foundation of his faith is not the person of Jesus Christ, but those facts about Him. If I am saved by a doctrinal system, if my belief in the facts my denomination has taught me is what redeems me, then anything outside of that system is threatening and suspect and shakes the foundations of my faith.

Again, as I said in the last chapter, the means of grace are not the end or goal of grace. The goal is a living relationship with Jesus Christ as Savior and Lord. It is He who saves. I can believe all the truths and all the facts about what God has done in and through Jesus Christ, His Son, and still not have a relationship with Him. I would still have only what the devils have. It really comes down to the question, Who is my God? If I find my security in the notion that my denomination is infallible, that its systematic theology is correct, and that this is what gets me to heaven, then I have a false god.

On the other hand, I have found that people who know Jesus Christ, who are secure in Him and who find that their relationship with Him is real—people who talk to Him and find that He talks to them—these people are not threatened when things which are biblical are discussed, even though they are outside the tradition which brought them their knowledge of the Lord Jesus.

Denominational loyalty, therefore, can be and often is prideful and idolatrous. Many, especially in doctrinally strict churches, have a misdirected faith. That is, the focus of their faith and the foundation of their security is what their church teaches rather than the person of Jesus Christ. God has used denominations, including the LCMS, but denominationalism, trusting in one's denomination and separating oneself from all others, is ungodly and unbiblical.

Early in my ministry I was flattered when members would come to me and ask, "What do we believe about that, Pastor?" I'm sure that this is usually an honest, sincere question from someone seeking information from one whom the individual respects for their biblical knowledge. However, it can reveal not only a biblical illiteracy caused by lack of a devotional life, but a lack of saving faith—as if an expert in the Scripture defines what a person believes. What do we believe? is an oxymoronic question. No one else can say what another person believes. One's belief system is the responsibility of the individual. The Christian faith is a gift of God the Holy Spirit, given through hearing, studying, reading, and/or meditating upon the Word of God. It always includes a personal trust in, knowledge of, reception of, and devotion to the Lord Jesus Christ. What do we believe? is the opposite of what the Bereans did. (See Acts 17:10–11.)

Is it Lutheran? If it's biblical, it's Lutheran. Be a Berean. Search the Scriptures to see if these things are true, and turn to Jesus who is the One who baptizes in the Holy Spirit! (See Matthew 3:11 and Acts 1:4–5.)

Chapter 8

THE LUTHERAN CHURCH—
MISSOURI SYNOD

URING THIS TIME of renewal in my life, I also
began to wrestle with the issue of how Lutheran
teaching and practice suggested that we relate to
Christians of other denominations. The Holy Spirit brings
the church together in unity, and God's love is poured into
our hearts through the Holy Spirit who has been given to
us. (See Romans 5:5.) That love was evident then and today
in gatherings of believers from all sorts of denominations
and non-denominational fellowships. When a recognized
teacher would come to our area, hundreds and sometimes
thousands would gather to hear him and worship the Lord.
Denominational labels were left at home, and the opening
worship times could last well over an hour. Worship was then
followed by the teacher, who could speak for another hour
or two. After praying together and ministering to individual
needs, sometimes for a few hours, many evening meetings
lasted well past midnight and into the early morning. Many
experienced miracles of physical and emotional healing
and deliverances from oppressive, evil forces. At times
there were things said that I didn't agree with (particularly

from the faith/prosperity stream of teachers, who I feel are unbalanced in their emphasis). However, I can't remember a meeting that didn't exalt the Scriptures as the Word of God and the Lord Jesus Christ as Savior and Lord, given by God's grace to be received by faith.

In spite of the love, joy, unity in Christ, nearness to God, spiritual growth, exaltation of the Father, and blessings experienced at these gatherings, I knew that my attending them could be a source of trouble for me in the Lutheran Church—Missouri Synod because of a teaching called unionism.

Unionism is largely a Missouri Synod term, whose definition has evolved from its first use in Prussia in the early eighteenth century. Its meaning at that time was connected with the efforts of the King of Prussia to commemorate the three hundredth anniversary of the Reformation by joining together the Lutheran and Reformed churches into one denomination by simply overlooking their doctrinal differences. Many Lutherans opposed this union and called those who favored it "unionists."

The meaning of the term has changed through the years from the joining together of two doctrinally different denominations to a narrower use of the word, applying it to all joint work, worship, or prayer among Christians of different denominations. Some older LCMS Lutherans may remember instructions about not bowing your head during the Lord's Prayer in public schools, lest you become a unionist with those who are not pure in their doctrine (the LCMS has historically been against prayer in public schools). The teaching even went so far as to restrict attendance to baccalaureate services (even for one's own class) and participation in the Boy Scouts. Great pain was caused in families who had saved relatives, even from other Lutheran denominations, that were forbidden to come to the Lord's Supper when visiting their loved ones because of their supposed lack of doctrinal purity.

In July of 1967 at the 47th convention of the LCMS held in New Your City, the Synod admitted that it had been misusing Scripture relative to its teaching on unionism. The convention approved a report of the Commission on Theology and Church Relations (CTCR) titled, "Theology of Fellowship." This document virtually removed all biblical support for the narrow interpretation of the doctrine of unionism. The report mentions that the passages used by many in the Missouri Synod in support of this interpretation were not used in that way by any of the church fathers, nor by Luther and the other early Lutheran theologians, nor by the Lutheran Confessions.[1]

One would expect that such an admission would bring a spirit of deep repentance and calling out to God and to Christians from other streams for forgiveness. After all, this misuse of the Word of God had caused disunity, false judgments, and an atmosphere of suspicion and sectarianism in the one body of Christ. It also caused the LCMS to join some of the fundamentalist denominations by constructing a false basis for fellowship, namely, purity of doctrine. The atmosphere did change somewhat, but sadly little, if any, repentance or change of heart occurred.

The LCMS's literature on the subject prior to the 1967 New York convention was quite negative, calling Christians of other denominations "belly servers and heretics."

However, literature written after 1967 became more positive. For instance, one source speaks of Roman Catholic and Baptist believers as being "brothers in Christ" of Lutheran believers.[2] It acknowledges that there is but one church and one Head, the Lord Jesus, and that all believers are in fellowship with one another by virtue of their fellowship with Him. Yet, surprisingly, this literature promotes the same false basis for Christian fellowship: agreement in all points of doctrine!

I believe this conclusion was reached by a misapplication of the difference between the unity *of* the church and the unity *in* the church: The literature points out that the unity of the church (*unitas*) is unity in the Spirit. It is the unity that is given by God. It is not a unity that needs to be arrived at by theological debate. It is a unity that all Christians have by virtue of their being Christian. Unity in the church (*concord*), on the other hand, is to be worked toward through ecumenical endeavors. The basis for our spiritual unity is simply that there is one Church, as we say in the Nicene Creed, "I believe in the one Christian (or catholic) and apostolic Church." But, says this literature, the basis for our external unity and therefore for any kind of fellowship is still that we must be in agreement on all points of doctrine.

Being a third generation LCMS pastor and loving my church body, I agonized over this issue with fear and trembling. I cried out to God. I searched the Scriptures. I sought out and questioned my brothers in the ministry. But through the Renewal, the walls were tumbling down. I had found loving, Christ-centered, theologically solid believers in

cally concerning the power and gifts of the Holy Spirit, seeing as I was going to have thirty or more theologians as members of the congregation. (The main passages concerning the charismata are in 1 Corinthians.) I made it a point to read, study, meditate upon, digest, diagram, pray about, and saturate myself with Paul's first letter to the church at Corinth.

As I did this I noticed that 1 Corinthians was also the only letter that talked about the Lord's Supper. In it is a verse that the LCMS has used to distance itself from other denominations. Through my study, I came to believe that verse does just the opposite.

First Corinthians 11:29 says, "For any one who eats and drinks [the Lord's Supper] without recognizing the body of the Lord eats and drinks judgment on himself." The traditional Lutheran understanding of that verse is that "recognizing the body" means discerning that the true body of Christ is in, with, and under the bread one receives in the Lord's Supper, thus affirming the Lutheran teaching of the real presence of Jesus in this sacrament. If this is true, that means anyone who doesn't believe in the real presence is an unworthy communicant (according to verse 27) and therefore Lutherans should surely not worship with them.

However, I am convinced that "recognizing the body" should have just the opposite result. This verse does not divide the church. It unites it!

A common thread runs through both 1 and 2 Corinthians. The church had terrible divisions among its members, little prideful groups that preferred one leader over another. These divisions were especially addressed in

1 Corinthians 11 through 14, where the Lord's Supper and the use of the gifts of the Spirit in public worship are discussed. His answer to both problems in these chapters is the spiritual unity of the body, to stop pridefully excluding people by instead lovingly including them. That's why chapter 13, the great love chapter, is in the middle of his treatise on the Spirit, His gifts, and their use in the body. It addresses the abuse of public displays of tongues as something to edify self rather to build up the body. Paul exhorts worshipers to stop being centered upon themselves and start loving one another.

This same issue was at the heart of the Corinthian's problem with the abuse of the Lord's Supper. They weren't concerned about one another. Instead, "each of you goes ahead without waiting for anybody else. One remains hungry, another gets drunk. Don't you have homes to eat and drink in? Or do you despise the church of God and humiliate those who have nothing?" (1 Cor.11:21–22).

Paul's solution for their abuse of the Lord's Supper is the same as his advice for their abuse of the Spirit's gifts: love. The issue is not a primarily doctrinal one; it's a matter of love, and Paul's solution is to use love to tear down the walls of division and include all who are members of the one body. Discern, see the body! Paul makes this clear when he goes into detail on correcting their divisiveness: "So then, my brothers, when you come together to eat, wait for each other. If anyone is hungry, he should eat at home, so that when you meet together it may not result in judgment" (1 Cor. 11:33–34). This passage clarifies what really makes someone an unworthy communicant: not discerning the body, not waiting for one another, and not loving one another. This makes sense theologically and medically. Theologically, we see that a consistent theme in the teachings of the Lord is the necessity to deal with relationship problems in the body of Christ. If you are going to church to worship the Lord and you remember that a brother has something against you, stop. Go and get reconciled with your brother and then come and bring your gift to the Lord. (See Matthew 5:23–24.) Or the other way around, if you have something against your brother, go speak to him alone about it, and if he listens to you, you have gained your brother back. (See Matthew 18:15). Get your marital relationships right or your prayers are going to be hindered. (1 Peter 3:7.) From a medical standpoint, Paul points out that the reason many of the Corinthians were "weak and sick, and some of you have fallen asleep [died]" (1 Cor. 11:30), is because they were receiving the sacrament without discerning the body. Prideful bitterness, resentment, and disunity will manifest themselves in physical symptoms.

POINT TWO

The 1967 LCMS Commission on Theology and Church Relations (CTCR) document on fellowship gives evidence that the early reformers did not come to the same conclusion as the LCMS literature.

In 1570 at the opening of the Synod of Sandomierz, in which representatives of Polish Calvinism, Polish Lutheranism, and the Unity of Bohemian Brethren participated, all held common worship. In the late sixteenth and seventeenth centuries, colloquies between Lutheran and Roman Catholic theologians were held repeatedly, all of which began with common worship. It was not until the Colloquy of Thorn that the practice was stopped, and then only because the Roman Catholics insisted that they alone conduct the devotions.[3]

Incidentally, years ago the Roman Catholic Church repented of that position and, unlike the LCMS, an overwhelming majority of bishops voted in Rome to ask forgiveness of their "separated brothers and sisters in the faith" around the globe for their divisive stand concerning joint worship.

The early reformers seemed to be following the example of the Lord Jesus Himself who, though He was fully aware of the error that existed among His fellow Jews, repeatedly worshiped in the temple right up to the week of His crucifixion. The same was true of the early believers in the Book of Acts who daily worshiped in the temple with the people who did not believe the same as they did. St. Paul, when on his missionary journeys, first went to the synagogues and worshiped with the Jewish people, who obviously did not possess the same doctrinal position he did.

POINT THREE

Donnie and I experienced something firsthand some years ago that greatly moved us relative to this issue. We were at a conference at Pastor Don Pfotenhauer's Way of the Cross Church in a Northern suburb of Minneapolis. Don was currently under fire from district officials for his charismatic leanings, so he and his congregation arranged to get leaders on both sides of the issue together to speak and respond to one another. It was Reformation Day, October 31. A Roman Catholic priest from an Eastern city talked about "celebrating the kingdom," that is, letting Jesus be Lord of your life and ministry. His intimate relationship with the Father, his love for the Lord Jesus, his understanding of salvation, and his life of joyful service to the poor in the inner city brought the walls down. Tape recorders, often a sign of renewal, were everywhere. When he was through, all you could hear was the sound of weeping. I was sobbing uncontrollably. After a while Don went to the podium to move on with the schedule, but he couldn't. He put his head down on the lectern and rejoined the crying chorus. After years of division, of talking about "those awful Catholics," there stood before us a humble, believing Roman Catholic priest in a Lutheran Church on Reformation Day convincingly demonstrating in word, attitude, and deed that he was a child of the heavenly Father and a precious brother. The Holy Spirit was bringing conviction and working repentance and deep sorrow for the antipathy once felt and the words of criticism once spoken. Negative feelings were being replaced by the same Spirit, with deep appreciation and love for this saint before us and for the unity of the whole body of Christ.

POINT FOUR

The mistake of making ends out of means is applicable to this issue also. Doctrinal unity, as important as it is, is not an end in itself, but is intended to deepen our relationship with God and bring about maturity in Christ. When it does that, it will aid the appropriation and expression of the spiritual unity that all Christians already have.

Doctrinal unity and biblical facts, in and of themselves, can be empty and meaningless. They are not the goal or demonstration that we have "arrived." If they were the goal, then the devil would have the prize since he knows and believes the doctrines. However, simple faith in Jesus, the faith that a child (who knows little of doctrinal formulations or theological language) can have, is the true basis for fellowship among Christians. As Luther says,

> If faith is real, it is a sure confidence of the heart and a firm assent, by which Christ is apprehended in such a way that He is the object of faith...in fact, not the object either, but, to put it this way, in such faith Christ Himself is present.[4]

Once again, the Word and sacraments are not ends in themselves. They are means of grace. They are the avenues through which God comes to us and we are drawn to Him. They are words to lead us to the Word. They are truths to lead us to the truth, the Lord Jesus Christ. All those who have been brought by these truths to the presence of Christ, to a relationship with *the* truth, the Lord Jesus, are children of the heavenly Father, dwelling places of His Holy Spirit, brothers and sisters of the Lord Jesus Christ, and our brothers and sisters. And they are to be treated as such.

I believe God is speaking to the whole body of Christ, saying, "Love me, love my kids. Stop these adolescent jealousies, judgments, words of gossip, rivalries, and putdowns. Grow up!" (See Ephesians 2 and 4; Romans 12, 14, and 15; 1 Corinthians 12:12–26 and 13; and Colossians 3:5–17.) Jesus indicated that the world would know that He is alive if His disciples would love one another. (See John 13:35 and John 17:21–23.) As the world looks at the church, it sees the scandal of people who say they believe in the one who is love, but don't show it to one another.

As I write this, my beloved LCMS is going through another time of tension as those who believe that they are the purest in doctrine are attacking others who, in their judgment, are not quite as pure. This is an even worse scandal: squabbling within a supposedly unified church body, a denomination in which our publishing house, many congregations and parochial schools, and almost all our colleges and seminaries are named *Concordia*, meaning "harmony." What a joke.

An earlier example of this tension occurred at the 60th Regular Convention of the Missouri Synod, which met in St. Louis in July of 1998. A resolution was brought to the convention to remove the Rev. Orval Mueller from his position as president of the Southern District of the church. I understand it was the topic of discussion at breaks, over coffee, meals, etc. What awful thing had Orval done?

In August, 1996, Pastor Mueller accepted an invitation to take part in the wedding of his niece, serving in that wedding with his brother-in-law (who was also an uncle of the bride) who was pastor of the host church in South Dakota. The problem was the church was not Missouri Synod. It was a member of the Evangelical Lutheran Church of America (ELCA). The president of the South Dakota District blew the whistle on Pastor Mueller.

However in 1998, this same South Dakota District president did what some in the LCMS (particularly the present leadership) believe is a terrible thing. He joined local Christian clergymen and laypeople in a prayer service when Spencer, South Dakota, was decimated by a terrible tornado. Most Christians would ask the obvious: Why, since biblically there is one body of Christ, one church, one faith, one God and Father of us all (Eph. 4:5–6), is it divisive to worship and help lead such a service with brothers and sisters in Christ? It would seem that it would be divisive *not* to do that. The official justification for the LCMS unionism teachings is that it is all in the name of love. It is unloving, they say, to pretend we are one with the Baptists when we are not. To worship with them would give them the impression that we all believe the same. That would be very unloving, and would keep them from searching out the truth we have.

It's as if almost everyone is in denial. We are no different than the crowd cheering at the emperor's beautiful, made-up suit of clothes. God weeps, and the world laughs. There is healing for this sickness: "recognizing the body" (1 Cor. 11:29, RSV). My prayer is that we would "wait for each other," as Paul admonishes us to do (1 Cor. 11:33). "Help us, Lord, to not charge ahead thinking of our own little group, eating, drinking, and enjoying ourselves. May we recognize the body. May we see Christ in our brothers and sisters—all our brothers and sisters, even those who may be behind us in Christian maturity and understanding. Help us love Christ in our brothers and sisters—all our brothers and sisters, even those who do not bear our denominational label. Move us to accept our brothers and sisters as members of the one body, the one faith."

For he himself is our peace, who has made the two
one and has destroyed the barrier, the dividing wall
of hostility, by abolishing in his flesh the law with its
commandments and regulations. His purpose was to
create in himself one new man out of the two, thus
making peace, and in this one body to reconcile both
of them to God through the cross, by which he put to
death their hostility.

—Ephesians 2:14–18

Live a life worthy of the calling you have received.
Be completely humble and gentle; be patient, bearing
with one another in love. Make every effort to keep the
unity of the Spirit through the bond of peace. There is
one body and one Spirit.

—Ephesians 4:1–4

The Lutheran Church—Missouri Synod

Chapter 9

FROM PAIN TO BLESSING

THE FAMILY WILDERNESS crisis I referred to earlier started in July with an unusually sharp pain in Donnie's womb. She knew immediately that something was wrong. Who would have believed that the pain would ultimately result in the adoption of two black babies into our white, Anglo-Saxon, protestant, middle class, Midwestern, small-town household? But it did.

The pain sent Donnie to the hospital, seven-and-a-half months pregnant, expecting our sixth child. She lay in the labor room and I, after calling the doctor, went home to take care of the rest of the children. At three a.m. the baby's heart stopped beating, the doctor was called, and a still-born son was delivered.

The same questions that I try to help answer when tragedy strikes the homes of the congregation now confronted our family: Why? Why do these things have to happen? It soon became evident, however, that an even greater question faced us. Would our family also be losing a wife and mother?

As Donnie's condition continued to become more serious, she was transferred to a large hospital in a metropolitan center some twenty-five miles away. There she was placed into an intensive care ward. Then came the parade of specialists, a new one every day, to try to discover why her blood pressure was fluctuating so rapidly and why she was becoming jaundiced. They suspected a deadly and very rare liver disease. In fact, her liver stopped functioning.

Despite excellent care and an all-out effort to bring about a cure, Donnie's condition steadily worsened. She became delirious and went into convulsions. I was with her for her last grand mall convulsion and helped hold her down. It was then that I accepted what the parade of specialists had intimated. Donnie—my wife—was dying. The baffled doctors confessed that they could do no more for her.

I and our congregation had been earnestly praying for her, but now I sought even more friends to pray. I knew the chairman of the Full Gospel Business Men's Fellowship International, a fellow Lutheran barber friend of mine. I telephoned him. "Ray," I said, "my wife is very sick, and I'd appreciate it if you would have a prayer for her in church Sunday." It wasn't long before he and his son-in-law, a missionary home on furlough from Africa, were in the hospital room. He wasn't going to wait until Sunday. He opened his Bible to the letter of James where, in the fifth chapter he read: "Is any one of you sick? He should call the elders of the church to pray over him and anoint him with oil in the name of the Lord. And the prayer offered in faith will make the sick man well; the Lord will raise him up."

Ray then proceeded to take out a vial of oil, anoint Donnie with it, and we all prayed. For the first time in many, many days, Donnie smiled! Then she fell into a deep sleep.

I stayed the night with her as I had done on other nights. The children were being cared for by members of our congregation, who so graciously showered us with their care, concern, material, and spiritual support.

The next day was Saturday. Donnie had been agitated, restless, and virtually out of her mind for a week. Now she continued to sleep peacefully. That night I went home to be with the children. On Sunday morning just before waking, I had a dream. I dreamed I was going to get married. I remember thinking in my dream, "Who would marry me with five children?" When it came time to march down the aisle with the bride, I walked down the aisle with my wife, Donnie! I then woke up.

I awoke, I dressed and drove to the hospital, all the while wondering about that dream. When I arrived, Donna was still asleep. I took her hand. She stirred a little. She opened her eyes and with a big smile the first words she said were, "It's our anniversary, isn't it?" Praise God! He had given back my wife. That was the meaning of my dream. She was dying, but He had given her back. It wasn't our anniversary, of course. That was a long way off. But it was the start of a new life together. God had brought her back and made us one again.

Two days later she was released from the hospital. She could have been released right away, but the physicians couldn't believe what had happened. They wanted to run some tests to be sure. The main doctor said, "I have never seen, in my many years of medical practice, a liver act like your liver. It's just impossible that one should recover the way yours did."

But it wasn't over yet. We had more to learn about God's faithfulness. Shortly after Donnie had gotten home from the hospital, she began to have terrible pain in her chest. A blood clot had settled in her lungs! She was immediately hospitalized, which she dreaded not only because of the pain and the separation from the family, but because she would have to face our family physician, whom she felt was at least partly responsible for our still-born baby boy. From what other doctors said, he apparently should have diagnosed her condition before its disastrous consequences developed.

She remembers how her anger simmered in her heart as, according to Donnie, he so nonchalantly visited her to examine her condition. The family, friends, and the congregation were all praying for her healing again, but she was praying about why this was happening and why she had to face this awful man. God made it clear that she had to face him so that she could forgive him. Finally, through the Lord's grace and mercy, she was able to completely forgive him, and with that forgiveness the anger was gone and she began to heal. God is faithful!

Upon returning home, we still felt a vacuum because of the absence of our long-expected baby. The doctor had said that she would have to have her female organs removed because she had what they called a couvelier uterus—a uterus that had been so saturated with blood that it would explode if a baby would be conceived. If this should happen, it would mean death for the baby and Donnie. After some discussion and prayer, we decided to look into the possibility of adopting a child, so we went to see the Lutheran Family and Social Service agency to learn more about the process. We also took the proper psychological tests and obtained the application forms. While we were there a number of photographs were shown to us, including pictures of two little black babies who had not yet been placed. The girl was a year old and the boy about seven months.

After returning home to pray and discuss this big step, we received word of the conference at Don Pfotenhauer's Way of the Cross Church in Minneapolis. We arranged for two college girls to stay with our children for three days while we attended the conference. There, one evening, Donnie knelt at the altar and prayed for healing. We firmly believed her prayer was answered.

Upon returning to Centerville, we decided to check with the doctor, one of the specialists who had been called in regarding her liver problems. At first he didn't recognize Donnie. After explaining who she was, he replied that seeing her was like seeing the dead come to live again. Upon telling him about our prayers for healing, he responded with an oxymoronic, "I believe in miracles, too, but in your case it's impossible."

The hysterectomy was scheduled for December 2, and at eight o'clock in the morning she was rolled into the operating room. It was expected that the surgery would take many hours, with many adhesions to separate because of the volume of bleeding that had occurred at and after the stillborn birth of our son. I went home to be with the children as we awaited completion of the procedure. An hour later at nine o'clock, I received a phone call from the hospital. "Please come to the hospital. The doctor would like to speak with you," the nurse said. My heart and stomach in turmoil and on the edge of panic, I rushed to the hospital to discover that Donna had indeed been healed. In the words of the doctor: " It's a miracle! I could see a spot where there may have been a hole, but it's all healed up. Her liver and all her organs are in excellent shape."

Later I learned from Donnie that before she was put to sleep she insisted that the doctor promise not to take anything out, including her appendix, unless absolutely necessary. She yearned to have another child. The doctor, who had twelve children, understood.

At home we were again faced with a decision. We had not yet made our application at the adoption agency. Now that we could have children in the usual way, should we go ahead with the adoption? Our family physician advised against any further pregnancies. Of course, many were telling us that it was his neglect of duty that had missed Donna's toxic condition and led to our baby's death.

We decided to pray about it. One night Donnie asked for a clear answer. She asked that if we were to have our own child, she would dream that she was having a baby. However, if we were to adopt, she asked Jesus to give her a dream that someone else was having a baby. To make it more sure, she asked that she would have three such dreams.

That night she had three dreams. God is faithful, indeed. In the first dream, one of her friends was having a baby. In the second and third dreams, women she didn't know were having babies. She awoke and told me. A short time later we sent our money and our application to the adoption agency.

Having five children of our own, we didn't want to deprive others of children who might have none, so we asked in the application for any child that the agency was having difficulty in placing. In fact, our hearts were drawn to one of the little black babies whose pictures we had seen. Both, especially the boy, were premature and had some possibilities of not-yet-discovered birth defects. The application was processed, the social worker visited with us, and all the problems of a multi-racial adoption were discussed, including the fact that they would be the only black residents of our little town (except for the many black students in the college). We prayed about it some more, and finally the adoption came through. We went to visit the babies, and they were both placed with us.

What a blessing they have been to us. It all started with pain, but has brought, as do all God's workings, the joy of His bounty and grace. We now had seven children—a holy number, and a sacred lot—David, Deanna, Deborah, Delisa, Dayna, Dona and Daniel.

Also significant to us were some coincidences: Dona's birthday is December 18, the same as my dad's, and Daniel's is May 23, the same as Donnie's sister Mary. Also, as I believe is true still today, adoptions don't become official until a trial period in the home ends. Dona and Daniel became official Dorpats on the birthday of the great emancipator Abraham Lincoln—February 12. The faithfulness of God in these things helped sustain us through coming difficulty, including hate mail we received regarding the adoption of our newest little ones.

Chapter 10

DIVINE APPOINTMENTS
AND CONFIRMATIONS

URING THESE THREE wilderness years that began in the fall of the year we arrived in Centerville, God also provided many fulfilling experiences of His grace and faithfulness.

Between the stillbirth of our baby boy and the adoption of Dona and Danny, my wife and I went through a time of grief. Because of her closer connection to him, Donnie especially mourned, sometimes thinking her loss was almost too much to bear. One day she went to one of the ladies meetings at church and an elderly woman shared about the flue epidemic that claimed thousands of lives early in the twentieth century. She didn't know this woman very well, except that she smiled a lot and seemed to have a lot of the joy of the Lord. She had six children and one by one they had died in that epidemic. Finally she was sitting in her bedroom, holding her sixth child, her baby, in her arms, rocking the little one in a rocking chair as she wept and cried out to God. Suddenly, light filled the room, though not from any window or bulb. It was the glory of the presence of the Lord. From the Word she knew that those children were with the Lord and she would see them again, but as she cried out to Him in her grief, the Lord had touched her with His manifest presence and she was comforted and even filled with the joy of the Lord.

Her testimony was a great comfort to Donnie, also. The presence of the Lord in that LCMS ladies meeting gave her the sure feet of a deer to climb her mountain of despair and stand with Him above the circumstances. Donnie came home virtually delivered from her sorrow.

The nature of my call to St. Mark's was also a confirmation of God's guidance and blessing. It was a joy to work with the junior high (confirmation age) and high school youth in the congregation, as well as to have frequent contact with students from the college. Because of the size of the congregation, it was impossible to visit each home of the members to get acquainted, as I had done in previous parishes. I did arrange a once-a-week "Evening with Pastor," an informal gathering with small groups of invited members to get to know them better and for them to get to know me. Refreshments were served and I shared John 6 with them, at the end of which I prayed a corporate version of the sinner's prayer, confessing sins, professing faith in Jesus and His atoning work on the cross, and asking Him to come into our hearts. I don't doubt that many came into a personal relationship with the Lord through these meetings.

Hospital calls were a daily duty for us. Ordinarily the senior pastor and I took turns. One day a call came in to visit a dying man. I found the room and, in it, a man connected to a myriad of tubes and buzzing, clicking medical machines. He was conscious, but unable to talk. I took his hand, introduced myself and asked him if he knew the way to heaven.

He was able to slightly shake his head in the negative. I asked him if he would like to know and he nodded his head yes. I shared the gospel with him and asked him if I could pray with him. Another yes nod. I encouraged him to make my words his own, thinking them in his mind as I prayed with him. As I finished the sinner's prayer and looked up, a big tear was running down his cheek. "Do you know that Jesus loves you and died for you?" Yes, he nodded. "Do you trust Him as your Savior?" Another yes. "Do you know He lives in your heart and you are a child of God on the way to heaven?" Another yes and more tears.

I walked out of that room on cloud nine and as I did, one of our St. Mark's members, a professor's wife and nurse at the hospital, saw me and exclaimed, "What are you doing in that room?" I explained that I had been called to visit the man and excitedly shared that he had received the Lord. She excitedly said, "Not with that man! His family had left strict instructions to not allow any pastor to visit him. They didn't want anyone to bother him!" I had gone into the wrong room! But it was no mistake. God once again showed Himself faithful.

During this time I was learning a bit about spiritual warfare. I believe the binding and loosing given with the keys of the kingdom have primarily to do with preaching law and gospel in order that sinners might repent and be forgiven. (See Matthew 16:18–19 and John 20:23.) However, in connection with spiritual warfare (particularly casting out demons), Jesus also speaks of binding the "strong man" (Matt. 12:29). He did this by taking authority over the demons and commanding them to leave. In taking authority over the devil and his hosts, Jesus spoke with authority to them, often using the sword of the Spirit, the Scriptures, as His weapon. (See Matthew 4:4, 7, and 10.) In all the Gospel accounts of Jesus sending out His disciples, He sends them out with His authority and power. He tells us in John that we will do the same works that Jesus did and, in fact, greater works, and that He sends us out as the Father has sent Him out. (See John 14:12 and 20:21.) Scripture also says that if we "resist the devil...he will flee from [us]" (James 4:7).

With those passages in mind, one Saturday evening when there was no one else around, I went into the sanctuary to pray. I also went to each pew and, while making the sign of the cross, I commanded all the powers of darkness, the hosts of wickedness in the heavenly places, the foul spirits, to be gone in Jesus name. I told them that Jesus is Lord, that through His cross and resurrection they are defeated—under His feet and under my feet, for I am seated with Him in the heavenly places. (See Ephesians 1:22 and 2:6.) I also blessed each pew, praying that the Spirit of God would bless each worshipper on the next day with His manifest presence and peace. I was keeping an eye out for anyone who might come in or look in from the narthex because I was not at all sure that this was what God wanted me to do. I felt I would look like a fool if anyone saw me. Because of this hesitancy on my part, when I was in the choir loft in the back of the church I stopped and laid hands on the organ, praying and proclaiming for an especially long time for confirmation that what I was doing was a good and godly thing. I asked that, if it were His will for me to pray in that way, He prompt the organist to tell me the next day that my sermon was good (the organist had never done this before).

After the last service the next day, I went down to my office on the lower level to hang up my robes before walking home for Sunday dinner. As I was taking them off, the organist walked in. He had come all the way down two flights of stairs from the balcony to find me and share how much he appreciated the sermon and the whole service. He couldn't stop talking. He followed me out the door and down the street to my home, although his was in another direction. All the while he continued telling me how God had blessed him during that service! It was a wonderful answer to prayer.

I believe there's a lesson here: we should spiritually clean God's house often. As believers we have authority over the powers of darkness. "Resist the devil and he will flee from you," is the promise of James 4:7.

Still, Donnie and I missed the freedom and vigor of the New Testament style of charismatic worship. One summer during this time, we had the opportunity to go to one of evangelist Herb Mjorud's family summer camps in Hungry Horse, Montana. It was a week of great joy and growth in the Lord. We floated home in Herbie, our tan Volkswagen van. Donnie said more than once, "I don't want to lose this feeling of closeness to the Lord. I'm going to have to find a way to have some regular private devotional time with the Lord." This wasn't going to be easy with seven children to care for and a busy, often absent, husband. How was she going to do it? Little did we realize a starving, crippled baby robin would provide the answer.

It was lying silent at my feet. We had arrived home and while the rest of the family was emptying Herbie, I went to check the oil in back and almost stepped on him. At first I thought he was dead. But as I reached down to pick him up, he opened wide his beak as only a hungry baby bird can do.

A box, some leaves, an old bird's nest, and excited children—could a bird survive under such conditions? Somewhere Donnie had read how to make "worms," so hard-boiled egg yokes mixed with bits of bread and milk were fashioned into worms that were then fed to our Robin every hour or so. To our family's amazement and delight, the robin not only ate those homemade worms, but also gladly received water from a baby spoon.

That first night Donnie set the alarm clock for six a.m. in order to get up and feed the bird. Faithful was the alarm (by my head). With no little disgust, I said to my wife, "Your dumb bird is waiting for his food." She bounded downstairs to discover that he was still alive, still hungry, and still ready to open his beak wide when she put anything close to it. She also noticed for the first time that he had a broken leg. He couldn't perch. He couldn't even stand. Can you put a splint on a robin's leg? What was going to happen to our bird? Donnie decided to just feed it and let nature take its course.

As the days went on, the bird grew and the leg healed. At first he was able to stand gingerly on one leg, perched on our finger or the edge of his box, but soon he was hopping around the back porch on both legs. Donnie also remembered reading that baby birds should be left outside as much as possible in order to get used to their natural habitat. Each night she would leave the bird under a bush, and each morning out he would scramble with loud and hungry chirpings to greet her and her "worms."

Soon our bird learned to fly. He had outgrown the box on the porch and chose instead to make his home in the trees around our house, yet whenever Donnie would come out to feed him, down he would fly and run across the lawn, tweeting and chirping excitedly to be fed. It was starting to get embarrassing. This full-grown bird apparently refused to feed himself. Donnie would lay seed or other food on the ground on a plate in front of him, but to no avail. He simply ignored that food and opened his beak, waiting to be spoon-fed. Donnie continued to feed him this way.

Finally there came a time when we wanted to go to a neighboring city to camp overnight and see the zoo. But could we? How about our bird? Would he survive? We prayed about it and decided that we would have to go if we were going to see the zoo before school started. You can't be tied down all your life by a robin that refuses to grow up.

The morning after our return from the zoo, our faithful alarm clock again jarred me from my peaceful sleep and sent Donnie downstairs and outside. Down came the bird, flying from the trees and running across the lawn to greet her. He had survived our three-day absence without our help. What a happy reunion!

From that time on, Donnie no longer had to feed him; he was no longer ours. But here's the point of this story: You know that six a.m. waking hour? It only takes a few minutes to feed a bird. For many years, the rest of the time between the feeding and when the children awakened was spent in prayer and Bible reading. God knew Donnie's desire and heard her prayer to find a time alone with Him in His sovereign providence and tender love. We believe that He provided a starving, crippled baby bird to answer her desire. I suppose that many would consider the whole thing a coincidence, but to us it was another demonstration of God's faithfulness.

Chapter 11

A TOUCH OF HEAVEN
IN CENTERVILLE

E XACTLY THREE YEARS after we moved to Centerville, three college students came to see me in my office. The two young men and young lady had been referred to me by a dear brother, the dean of the chapel at the college, with whom Donnie and I coincidently had shared about our experience with the presence and work of the Holy Spirit. The students had come to him with a request for prayer and praise meetings. Because of their experience with the Holy Spirit back home in the New York City area, they desired to participate in freer, what they called "New Testament-type," worship and fellowship. The three wilderness years were over, just as the prophecy had said.

Right away we began weekly charismatic prayer meetings, which continue to this day. Our home became a house of prayer, also in answer to prophecy. Except for a brief relocation during the storm before that dreadful voter's meeting, our home was the location for those prayer meetings for eight years.

During that first school year after we began the meetings, the attendance at these gatherings included just Donnie, myself, and these three students. Very often even I was not able to attend, partly because our beloved friend, the senior pastor at St. Mark's, preached his farewell sermon. He had accepted a call to serve a congregation in a neighboring state, leaving me as the only called pastor on staff at St. Mark's. I was busy enough before he left, but now the buck stopped with me.

The meetings exploded during the second school year. Fifteen students attended our first prayer meeting. The next week there were thirty of us and the next, sixty. Young people involved in the Jesus movement in California were hearing a call from the Holy Spirit to full-time service in the church and enrolling in the college, as were students from the East Coast and the Ann Arbor area who had been touched by the renewal in the Roman Catholic Church. They came and, in turn, were inviting their friends to come and see what God was doing at the Dorpat home. We had wall-to-wall students in our small living room sitting on every available chair, on the floor, in our adjoining kitchen and the small den, our "upper room" (it was a three inch step up from the living room), as well as on the stairs leading up to our second floor bedrooms.

Donnie and I will forever be grateful to God for those years of renewal at Centerville and the way He showed His faithfulness to us through it. The prayer meetings were unbelievably blessed. The students had such a zeal for the Lord, such joy in the Spirit, and such freedom to worship and minister to one another. The meetings would begin at eight p.m. and last for two or three hours, followed by prayer and fellowship with one another that sometimes lasted until two or three o'clock in the morning. Freshmen, who had an eleven p.m. weekday curfew in the dormitories, were getting into trouble, not because they were partying or in the back seat of some car but because they lost track of the time in worship, prayer, and fellowship!

In the LCMS 1998 Synodical Convention, a major move was made to centralize authority in order to insist on conformity, not only in doctrine but in practice. More simply put, things like the form of our worship services and our liturgies were now all to be the same each Sunday. In spite of the fact that the Augsburg Confession, the Apology of the Augsburg Confession and the Formula of Concord (some of our Lutheran foundational formulations of doctrine) all clearly say that "it is not necessary for the true unity of the Christian church that ceremonies, instituted by men, should be observed uniformly in all places,"[1] and "churches will not condemn each other because of difference in ceremonies."[2] I take that to mean that those in authority shall not condemn local congregations for creative worship services. It appeared to me like another appearance of the same legalism which Jesus battled and which has cursed the church for centuries.

I wish our present-day leaders could have dropped in on our prayer meetings. The forms and ceremonies that took place there in our home went back beyond the early traditions of the Missouri Synod, beyond the liturgies suggested by Martin Luther, and beyond the time of Constantine. Our meetings reflected the days following Pentecost as the believers, filled with the Holy Spirit, met both in the temple and daily in their homes to break bread together, pray, and to worship the Lord. Rufus Jones, a non-charismatic Christian philosopher and historian describes that early group of believers. (All parenthetical Scripture references have been added by the author.)

> There was a band of disciples at Ephesus before Paul came, but they did not form an *ecclesia,* in Paul's sense, until the Holy Spirit came upon them and they spoke with tongues and prophesied like the other church groups. [Acts 19:1–7.] While this mystical stage of primitive Christianity lasted the members had a common experience. They were fused. They were baptized into one Spirit. [1 Corinthians 13:13.] They ate a community meal—all partaking together of one loaf and altogether drinking of the one cup. [1 Corinthians 10:17.] This love meal was eaten with an awakened memory of Christ's last meal with his friends and with a fresh palpitating sense of the invisible presence now with them. It was both sacramental and mystical in the true sense and it was a powerful, integrating experience.
>
> There was no rigid system. Custom had laid no heavy hand upon anyone. Routine and sacred order had not yet come. There was large scope for spontaneity and personal initiative. Persons and gifts counted for everything. The procedure was fluid and not yet patterned, static and standardized. There was a place for the independent variable. The fellowship was more like a family group than like the church as we now call it. Love rather than rules guided it and everything was unique. Nothing was repeatable.
>
> The exercises, if we may judge by the glimpses we get from Acts and Corinthians, were of a sort that favored mystical experience. They were largely born

out of and developed to fit personal and community experience. No leader dominated the group meetings. No one person was essential. The little body met as a community of the saints and, as Paul said, where the Spirit is, there is liberty, not bondage and routine. The exercises were charismatic that were due to the display of spiritual gifts possessed by those who were present. [1 Corinthians 12 and 14.] The leading gift was prophecy which consisted of a spontaneous utterance of a message believed to be inspired by the Spirit, by those who had formed a well-stored sub-conscious life to draw from. It was often illuminating and effective, "edifying" as Paul would say. Some-times the flooded lives broke forth in hymns. [Ephesians 5:18–20 and Colossians 16–17.] Sometimes they altogether called out "Abba" or "Maranatha" or groanings that could not be uttered. [Romans 8:26.] And sometimes one or more broke into emotionally loaded unutterable utter-ance, that is, tongue-speaking.

There was also a greatly heightened moral power. They walked in the Spirit. They bore the fruit of the Spirit: love, joy, peace, long-suffering, kindness, good-ness, faithfulness, meekness, self-control. [Galatians 5:22–23.] The picture in 1 Corinthians 6:9–11 shows like a flash of lightning what their lives had been before they were washed and sanctified. And in his epistle to them he calls them letters of Jesus written by the Spirit being transformed into his image from glory to glory by the Spirit of the Lord. [2 Corinthians 3:17–18.] He, at least, expected them to live in a spirit of coopera-tive love which is patient and kind, long-suffering and gentle, unprovoked; which believes and hopes and endures everything. [1 Corinthians 13:4–7.]; and which as an inward, working and creative force would make them a single body, a unified fellowship.[3]

In so very many ways, this passage describes both the life of worship and fellowship of the early church and the events of the prayer meetings in our home, even though Rufus Jones never visited our gatherings, had to my knowledge no firsthand experience in free worship outside of reading the Scriptures, and wrote the above long before the time of today's Charismatic Renewal. I have only one bone to pick: "this mystical stage of primitive Christianity" was neither primitive nor particularly mystical. It was concrete and very up to date. The Holy Spirit of God was manifesting His presence among His people through His blessed gifts, and they were bearing His fruit: love, joy, and peace. (See Galatians 5:22–23.) Nor was it just a stage, a transient period that shortly and forever disappeared from the scene. In one form or another, it has existed throughout the church's history, although at times, like in the Dark Ages when the gospel was virtually lost, it was rare.

This time of renewal was incredibly exciting. Again and again, week after week, God graced our prayer gatherings with clear manifestations of His presence and blessing. Many of the students who came to the meetings were music majors who brought along their instruments, talents, and voices. The joyful singing of praise and worship, a kind of spontaneous spiritual jam session, would sometimes go on for an hour or more. At first no hymnals or song sheets were needed; we just sang the old psalms, hymns, and spiritual songs that we all knew by heart. But as students came back from summer, Christmas, and Easter breaks, they brought beautiful compositions they had learned at their local prayer meetings, and we began to learn and "sing…new song[s] to the Lord" (Ps. 33:3, 144:9, and 149:1). These new spiritual songs and hymns were traveling around the country without sheet music or human design.

Sometimes during the worship, the whole group would begin to lift their voices in spontaneous melodious praise and worship. Each would sing with his or her own melody and lyrics, in English or in tongues, but the individual songs would blend together in such beautiful harmony that it seemed like the angels were joining in. I believe we were— and still are today—singing in the Spirit as Paul said in 1 Corinthians 14:15. God was putting "a new song into our mouths" (Ps. 40:3).

Also without human direction, each student would come ready to share a hymn, a reading from Scripture, a teaching from the Word, a testimony, and sometimes, though rarely, a word of prophesy or tongue and interpretation. It was 1 Corinthians 14:26 all over again: "What then shall we say, brothers? When you come together, everyone has a hymn, or a word of instruction, a revelation, a tongue or an interpretation." These kids were in their late teens or very early twenties, but they displayed a maturity and wisdom that amazed Donnie and me.

The Spirit was birthing a movement that was both nationally and internationally unified and unifying, yet without human plans or committees. It just seemed to happen. Even the teachings that were coming forth in the local areas were naturally forming part of a national pattern. First the primary topic was the Spirit, the gifts, and the nature of praise and worship; then marriage and the family; then the kingdom of God; then the body of Christ, its unity, its nature as the loving family of God; then believers as a community, a unified organism; then local and world outreach. There were no centrally produced study guides or directives, and no programs or plans from headquarters. Rather, from on high, the same Spirit who raised Christ from the dead dwelling in these mortal bodies was giving life and quiet, grace-filled direction to each local expression of His universal body. What faithfulness!

Traveling teachers who spoke in churches, auditoriums and, often, in home meetings were yet another heavenly blessing that God sent us periodically. These brought spiritual growth and another expression of the great unity in the Spirit that all believers have. One such man was Charles Schmidt from Minnesota (currently at Immanuel's Church in Silver Springs, Maryland), who often came to our home and shared from the Word. Though not a Lutheran, he is a wonderful, inspiring Bible teacher and lover of the Lord Jesus. He did much to help establish our community of believers on a biblical basis.

There were many other teachers that we came to know. Art Katz, a Messianic Jew and author of the book, *Ben Israel*, made a profound impression on St. Mark's Church. He had been a man whose search for meaning and purpose in life had led him through the formal and personal study of the philosophies of the world—philosophies that didn't fulfill his hunger. Finally he came to know the Lord Jesus as his Messiah, and his soul was satisfied. He had just returned from Europe, where he had proclaimed the gospel through philosophical debates with student activists, agnostics, and revolutionaries at numerous universities there. We learned he was going to be speaking at a large city not far away, so we went to hear him. After his inspiring and challenging talk, I went up and asked him if he would be willing to come and talk at the college at Centerville. He agreed and, although at such late notice I was unable to get a convocation scheduled in the auditorium, the administration did give permission for him to speak in the Student Center. I also scheduled him to speak at my noon Kiwanis luncheon.

Art came to our home and he, Donnie, and I visited and prayed together. I gave him directions on how to get to the luncheon because I was going to pick up some professors I had invited to be my guests that day. Art and I sat together as we ate our meal. I told him that I was going to introduce him, and I wondered aloud if he was going to share about his ministry to the college students in Europe and America. He responded, "I don't know yet." As the time drew nearer and nearer for introductions, I asked him many times again what he was going to speak on. Each time he replied, "I don't know yet."

Finally the time had come, and I rose to introduce him. All of us were concerned about the radical movements, demonstrations, and turmoil that were happening on the campuses at that time. I'm sure there was in most all of us a certain self-righteous indignation at these rebellious youth. So in my introduction I told these men, thirty of Centerville's leading citizens, about how Art had been debating these youth in universities in Europe and America, also mentioning that Art was a converted Jew.

To polite applause, Art took his place at the podium. His first words were, "I am not a converted Jew, I am a completed Jew. I have come to know my Jewish Messiah." He then began to pointedly address the crowd of white, Anglo-Saxon Protestants before him. His message was that the radical youth movements, as troubling as they were, were not nearly as problematic to God as the apathetic, hypocritical, pharisaic, self-satisfied middle class male who may have a nodding acquaintance with the Creator, but whose real gods are money, upward mobility, and social and/or political power and prestige. With great passion and, I felt, Spirit-inspired zeal, he used the Word of God as a two-edged sword to open up our hearts to the truth about ourselves. In Lutheran language, he proclaimed the law in all its severity. Then he told them about Jesus and how they could come to know and follow God by trusting Him and inviting him to take over their lives. I was shaking and near tears, and I noticed some others were too. I didn't know if theirs was rage or repentance. He then led them in the sinner's prayer and was seated.

As I drove my guests back to the College Administration building, the car was mostly silent. Before I left the three theologians off, I asked them what they thought. They weren't too impressed. One said, "There's a time and place for everything, and that was not the time or place for that." Another felt it was not a very good way to witness to people. As I drove the art professor to his home, he told me, "Dave, that was great! I loved it!"

I soon learned how great it was. About half of the Kiwanians were members of St. Mark's, and many of them were infrequent in their church attendance. I noticed that some of those lukewarm believers were now attending every Sunday and were smiling a lot more.

That evening the large lounge of the Student Center on campus was crowded in anticipation of Art's address. Word had gotten around. Half the football team was there. Art shared how God had gotten hold of him. As he talked about his struggles, the Holy Spirit's faithful intervention and the uncompromising call of God upon his life, the lounge became a holy sanctuary of the Lord's manifest presence. A number of the football players were weeping uncontrollably. I put my arm around the shoulder of one and asked him if I could be of help. He said he was weeping for his classmates and teammates who were missing the address. Art again closed with the sinner's prayer and a prayer of re-commitment to the Lord Jesus and His claim upon our lives. The whole day was another wonderful testimony.

Chapter 12

MORE DIVINE APPOINTMENTS
AND CONFIRMATIONS

P RAYER WAS AN obvious part of our weekly meetings. We communed with God not only in words and songs of adoration and thanksgiving, but we talked to Him in petitions and intercessions. He was faithful and answered in many miraculous ways, confirming His presence and call upon our little group. (See Romans 15:18–19; Mark 16:20; Hebrews 2:3–4.) The emphasis of the Spirit among us was more on worship, community, and His faithful guidance than on healings and other miracles, but that didn't thwart our enthusiasm.

In my recollection, the closest thing to a mighty miracle of healing came after one of our meetings when our pet white kitten, the offspring of our long-time house cat, Daisy, was playing with the students in the living room. We commented to the students that she was deaf. From what we had heard from others, there is a strain of white cats in that area of the country who are often born deaf. To demonstrate that the kitten was deaf, we had everybody quiet down, tip-toed up behind the cat, and loudly clapped our hands behind her head. She didn't jump, turn, or respond at all. She would react from someone stomping on the floor as she felt the vibrations, but did not react at even very loud noises. Well, the students immediately went into action, gathered around her, laid hands on her, and prayed earnestly for her. They might have even anointed her with oil, I don't remember. We smiled and kind of shook our heads. A day or so later, however, we noticed that our little white kitten could hear.

There were other wonderful things that God did that warmed our hearts and brought great joy and praise to His name. Not the least of these was the tremendous love and unity that existed among us. As Rufus Jones said of the early church, we were fused, bonded together, made to be one family through the blood of Christ and His presence in and among us. I believe that, especially in the core group, we would have all given our lives for one another and still would.

That unity was pictured in a vision (or dream, I don't remember which) that one of the students shared one evening at our meeting. He saw a bundle of wheat gathered together in a sheaf, such as you see at harvest festivals or Halloween. Then the stalks of grain shot out of the bundle and went all over the nation and world. He felt that our group was the bundle of grain and God was going to send us out. That certainly seemed logical since all of the students were preparing for full-time ministry in the church and many would soon be graduating and going on to the seminary or receiving calls to teach at one of our denomination's many parochial elementary or secondary schools. Later on, the students noted that in the Bible the Lord sent out laborers two by two. This truth was added to the vision of the bundle of grain, and we wondered how that would happen. Before the third year was over the mystery was solved: twenty of the group were engaged or on the verge of getting engaged. And they have gone out around the world. We still hear from them or about them in cities from coast to coast and in many foreign countries where they are faithfully building the kingdom.

One of the tests mentioned in Scripture concerning the validity of the Spirit's presence and work is whether or not there is fruit being borne. A stag party that the young men had for one of those grooms reminded me of an experience I'd had a few years earlier at Christ the King in Coeur d'Alene. I had gone to visit a young man who had been confirmed. He had stopped coming to church, and I was encouraging him to return to our Sunday fellowship. He looked me in the eye and said, "You know, nobody enjoys going to church." What a contrast that attitude was to these young men and their stag party. The party consisted of them gathering together in a dormitory room to worship and praise the Lord and lay hands on the groom to pray for him and his marriage. They then read portions of Scripture about marriage to the groom from the Bible and from Larry Christianson's book, *The Christian Family*. These young people couldn't get enough of church.

In fact, the Renewal spilled from our house onto the campus of the college that was right across the street from our home. The students told their friends and roommates about what the Lord was doing, and groups began praying together and studying Scripture together all over campus. We had new brave or just plain curious students at almost every prayer meeting.

These students, the vast majority from strong Lutheran homes, many of them preacher's or parochial school teacher's kids, faced the same cultural and theological barriers that had caused me to study for three years before embracing the Renewal. Although Billy Graham and other Christian leaders had predicted a few years earlier that the study and experience of the Holy Spirit would increase greatly in the church during this time in our nation's history, for the most part and for most Christians, the Holy Spirit was still the forgotten person of the Trinity at this time. We can relate to the Father because most of us have fathers. We can relate to the Son. Jesus became a human being and walked this earth with us—just like us except without sin. But who is the Holy Spirit? A Yale divinity student about this time described him as "an oblong blur." We are less able to relate to the Holy Spirit. He seems ethereal, hazy, vaporous, and difficult to grasp. Holy or not, He's described as spirit, and people in our Western culture are mostly uncomfortable and sometimes fearful of such things.

It seems to me that the content of Scripture concerning the Holy Spirit is not primarily theological terminology that would enable us to describe or define Him. Scripture rather primarily and simply reports on how He manifests himself. That's what the students in our prayer meetings were talking about to their friends. They were telling them that God, the Holy Spirit, was healing people and giving His gifts in our day, such as tongues, interpretation, and prophecy. That's also scary to a lot of people.

I remember talking with one of our student leaders about these fears and he said, "They are afraid that someone is going to take over their lives." That statement about knocked me over. I began to laugh and laugh. It's doubly true! That is why many are afraid, and that is exactly what God wants to do. He's not here to take sides in theological and denominational debates. He's here to take over. Christian maturity is not measured in what you know, but whom you know and the degree to which He has laid hold upon your life. Paul confessed that "the love of Christ controls us" (2 Cor. 5:14, RSV). That is the work of the Holy Spirit.

Lutherans are primarily focused on what God did two thousand years ago and that He is high and lifted up in glory and majesty (i.e., far away). Historically, our church buildings, along with most of Christendom, were primarily built along Old Testament worship lines. The people sat in rows facing but at a respectful distance from the chancel area with its altar, the focal point of worship. Many customs gave you the impression that this area was like the holy of holies in the temple. The altar rail served as a kind of barrier curtain. Ordinarily no one went beyond it except the pastors or elders who helped with communion. When the pastor or other worship leader approached the altar, he bowed in reverence toward this symbol of the presence of God. Children did not play in the chancel area at any time, during or outside of services. A quiet reverence and order was expected by anyone who entered the sanctuary (the meeting hall). Everything was written down and either spoken or sung in unison. Even for those who led the service, most everything they said was prepared and printed out ahead of time, much of it preserved and handed down from centuries past.

As far as I'm concerned, these are good traditions. They

certainly instilled in me a reverence for God and a feeling of continuity and foundational solidarity with the historic church. But there is more to worship, both in the Old Testament and especially in the New Testament. In the New Testament, the presence of God is no longer in an enclosed area behind a barrier curtain. God Himself tore that curtain from top to bottom when Jesus died, signifying that we no longer need sacrifices and high priests to approach God. All believers are priests and have, through the once-and-for-all sacrifice of the blood of Jesus, free access to Almighty God. In fact, by teaching us to pray *Abba* (which means "father"), I believe Jesus virtually invited us to climb up into our Father's lap. Even to the psalmist, God encouraged a hugging relationship with Himself. (See Psalm 91:4.) How much more freely should we who have known the tender mercies of our Father in the grace of our Lord Jesus Christ be able to enjoy, dance, clap hands, and let go of our inhibitions as we celebrate with worship and adoration in the loving presence and, yes, embrace of our great God.

Corporately and individually, we are the temple of the living God. (See Ephesians 2:21–22; 1 Corinthians 3:16–17 and 6:19; 2 Corinthians 6:16). The church is not a building. *We* are the church. *We* are the holy of holies! In most Lutheran buildings of worship in the past, the organ and choir were placed in a balcony at the rear of the sanctuary so that they would not distract from the center of worship. Leaders of worship wore robes in order to hide their clothing, lest that be a distraction. But God does not live in an altar; He lives in us. It is no distraction to watch the saints of God singing or playing instruments to the Lord. They are the residents of

God. They are vessels containing the focus of our worship, the triune God.

We are also the family of God, brothers and sisters in Christ Jesus. Almighty God is our Abba Father, Jesus is our blessed Brother, and the Holy Spirit is the presence that makes us all one family. (See Ephesians 4:3–6.) When a healthy family gets together after a time apart, it is anything but quiet and serious. Joyful greetings, laughter, hugs, and kisses abound. Growing up in our formal, reverent services, I remember that the worst thing one could do was to make any kind of mistake that would in any way disrupt or distract from what was going on. What shame and embarrassment you would feel if you dropped the offering plate, for instance, fainted, started to sing the wrong verse, sneezed at the wrong time, or any number of other mistakes.

It was the sainted Father Dennis Bennett who years ago spoke to my heart on this topic by describing the difference between emotionalism and an honest, godly expression of one's heartfelt convictions and feelings. He said that emotionalism is like a football stadium full of people in the stands jumping up and down in excitement, clapping their hands, and shouting with joy over an empty field. But when the stands erupt in uninhibited, loud, joyous celebration as the line makes its blocks, the quarterback is right on target, the end catches the ball and zigzags down field for a touchdown, that's an honest expression of understandable excitement. When you see a handful of people sitting in the stands stony-faced, serious, or bored, you assume they're fans of the other team or that they don't know what's going on.

Well, our God is far greater and more exciting than any sports event. His presence is more real. His life in us is more motivating to celebration and sheer, uninhibited expressions of joy and adoration than any activity this world can offer. What else should be more exciting and fulfilling than gathering as the family of God to hear from Him and worship Him? How strange for people to sit in church somber or disinterested. Don't they see what's going on? God is present, speaking, and acting.

There's no doubt in my mind that our Lutheran emphasis on strict formalism with its lock-step repetition of the same words and forms Sunday after Sunday is imbalanced, as is our one-sided emphasis on the transcendence of God (I've heard seminary graduates say that a professor warned them to steer clear of the concept of "Christ in us"); our use of only four hundred-year-old music; our insistence on a reserved, reverent, emotionally restricting atmosphere; and our "great gulf" mentality between clergy and laity.

This historic imbalance has resulted in an odious, but almost universal tradition in the LCMS, one that is unwritten and greatly disliked by pastors and leaders. It was illustrated to me at a church I served temporarily while their congregation sought another pastor. I almost lost it at the first service I conducted in this congregation. The church building was quite large, located, along with a closed parochial school and an empty parsonage, out in the country a few miles from Centerville. Their custom was that the pastor stayed in the vestry during the first hymn and then came out to lead the service. During the last verse of the hymn, I walked out and faced the altar for the invocation. I then turned to face the congregation for the first time and almost broke down. Here were all these pews stretching to the right, left, and to the back. At first it seemed that no one was there, but as my eyes traveled to the rear of the church, there they all were, huddled together in the back rows under and in the balcony. I noticed this phenomenon at many churches. People would greet one another on the church steps with warmth, love and good cheer. But once they crossed the imaginary line—it could be at the doors that go into the sanctuary or the one between the last two pews—their faces changed from pleasant, relaxed, and cheerful to somber, stiff, and sometimes even sour. Through the years, Lutherans got the message being sent by the church: God is so transcendent that He is well nigh unapproachable. We are such sinners and He is so holy that we better not get too close. The Lutheran tradition faithfully followed by the vast majority is to sit in the back.

It seems to me that the New Testament describes celebrative, inclusive, enthusiastic worship, where all who gather contribute and many share what the Spirit is saying through them, all to build up the body. (See 1 Corinthians 12–14, Ephesians 5:18–20, and Colossians 3:16.)

I love the way a fellow Renewal in Missouri founder pastor Herb Mirly describes a worship service. He says that sometimes we give the impression that in a service the actors (or players) are the pastors, musicians, and other leaders. Their coach is God and the congregation is the audience. Not so, Mirly says. The people are the players, the coaches are the pastors and other leaders, and the audience is God. We all come to actively worship the Lord. Our worship is directed to him and him alone. The leaders are there to help us, and

God is the object of it all. Herb once encountered a lady who commented to him on the way out of church that she didn't like one of the hymns that had been sung that morning. He gently told her that while he didn't want to hurt her feelings, the hymn had not been picked for her, but for God.

If there's one place you should be able to relax and be yourself without worrying about protocol or rigid human rules, it's when you're with the family in the embrace of the Father. If there's one place you should not worry about dropping the offering plate it's at church, where the Father and your brothers and sisters accept you unconditionally.

It's true that the foundation of everything is what God did two thousand years ago, and that can never be overemphasized. It's true that He is our Father who is in heaven, high and lifted up in majesty. Especially in a society such as ours where it is popular to be irreverent, we need to stand in great and holy awe of Him who is the "wholly other," immeasurably greater, wiser, magnificent, mighty, etc. than we are or ever will be. But at the same time He invites us to call Him Abba, Daddy. Because of Jesus He is not only completely approachable, He is nearer than our hands and feet, more real than what we can touch and taste, and more exciting than anything anybody, anywhere, or at any time could ever imagine.

The students from our meetings were describing to their friends a God who is now palpably near and doing things in friends' and neighbors' personal lives. They described a God of present-tense healing, deliverance, help, and transformation. I remember reminding these students who were trying to help shed light on their friends' fears about God that the symbol of the Holy Spirit is a dove. Could anything be less threatening than a dove? God is awesome beyond belief, but more approachable because of Jesus than anyone else in the whole universe. What a wonder it was and a confirmation of God's presence and blessing to see these inquiring students become free in the Spirit to celebrate the presence of God and express the almost inexpressible joy of their salvation.

Another confirmation of His guidance was that we learned some more things about spiritual warfare during this time. Donnie and I were like most married couples—we had our differences. In fact, we were about as alike and humanly compatible as a dog and a cat, but through the years we have learned to appreciate our unique qualities. As the French say, Vive la différence. We became convinced as we counseled and related to myriads of couples all over the USA that married couples were never supposed to be compatible. How could one be compatible with someone so completely different in so many ways? But God planned it that way. We all have rough edges in our lives. Marriage is a great way to get them ground down and, in the grinding, to mature. As one teacher put it, we were "divinely designed to grind." Marriage is growing up time—growing up into the image of Christ.

We began to notice that on the day our evening prayer meeting was scheduled, something seemed to happen to get Donnie and I going at one another just before the students were about to arrive. It took quite a while but, spiritually sensitive giants that we were, we finally figured out that maybe we were being harassed because the enemy didn't like what we were doing. The next time the air got a little tense before the meeting we stopped, joined our hands, prayed, and took authority over the old evil foe. We resisted the devil and he fled from us. He no longer even tried to get at us during that time because he knew we would pray, and he doesn't want that.

One day a student dropped by my office and said that he felt the Lord wanted us to wash one another's feet at the meeting that evening. I smiled and said something like "we'll see," my usual response to our children when they were proposing something I wasn't too interested in. Another one dropped by a little later with the same suggestion. I wondered what was going on over at the college. My feet and toenails are the ugliest on the planet, so I wasn't impressed by the idea of a foot washing.

That evening something happened that had never happened before. We always began the meetings with a long time of worship and praise, which led into a free time of sharing what God had been saying to us through our devotional life in the Word. Usually one or two would give a more extended teaching from Scripture during that time. But this evening, before we could get started into worship, one of the students began to talk about humility and how he felt God wanted us to humble ourselves before him. Then Donnie, who I had not told about the two students who came to see me at the office, spoke up and said she had been reading in John 13 about Jesus washing the disciple's feet. We all turned there in our Bibles and she gave a little teaching on that section.

The Scripture speaks about needing two or three witnesses to confirm something and here we had four so far. My stubborn, selfish will was broken, and I told the group about the two who had come to me that afternoon. We got out the pans from the kitchen and the towels from the linen closet and had a foot washing. Bathed with prayer, preceded by a time of repentance, and followed with thanksgiving, worship and praise, it was a mountain top experience. And no one laughed at my feet, though I'm sure there was an increased admiration for my wife's tolerance and loyalty.

At the end of the evening, I found that none of the four witnesses had talked to each other about the topic. They had each been moved independently to bring the subject up. God is faithful.

These kinds of things happened again and again among us back then, and they have continued to happen in congregations we've been involved with since. Because of the busyness of the pastoral ministry and some procrastination, I often did not finish my sermon preparation until after midnight on Sunday morning. Without knowing what I was going to preach about, the musicians, in prayer, picked exactly the right music, and often a word or two of prophecy came from the body before the sermon that fit the message perfectly.

Another example of such tender, loving care and guidance from the Spirit happened after we had been studying the importance of the diversity of the body of Christ. We had been researching the fact that each member of the body of Christ has been equipped to fill a particular place in that body. In keeping with the Reformation truth that all believers are priests who have places of service or ministry, we were exhorted to seek the Lord about our place. Where did we fit? What was our ministry or ministries? Donnie took that to heart, and while ironing clothes one day she called out to

God and asked what her ministry was. She felt that He said one word to her: "peace."

"Peace?" she thought to herself. "I've never heard of that as a ministry. Or does God mean that I should have peace about this?" She put down her iron, picked up her Bible, and proceeded to do something that I do not recommend at all. She opened her Bible up at random and the first verse she laid her eyes upon had in it the word *peace*. She thanked the Lord and closed and opened it again. The same thing happened, *peace* and again, *peace*. She did it once more and opened to Psalm 122:6–8: "Pray for the peace of Jerusalem: 'May those who love you be secure. May there be *peace* within your walls and security within your citadels.' For sake of my brothers and friends, I will say, 'Peace be within you'" (emphasis added). There it was, three times in three verses. But she still didn't have an answer to her question. Was peace her ministry, or should she just have peace about the question? Then the phone rang. It was a student from the college. She was troubled and wanted to talk. Donnie invited her over, listened to her, counseled, and prayed with her. As the student was leaving, she turned to Donnie and said, "Thank you, Mrs. Dorpat. I have such peace!"

At the end of our prayer and praise meeting that week, most of those who had been coming regularly stayed after as they usually did for munchies, fellowship, and further prayer. As I mentioned, we were all very close. That evening, a few of them shared an experience they had that week. They were enjoying each other's company in one of the dormitory rooms and talking about the brothers and sisters when they started to liken each of them to a biblical character. It all started in fun, but turned into an exciting time filled with the manifest presence of God. Before the day was over, they had given each of the members of this core group a biblical name and passage to go with it. That evening they shared them.

"John is like a Jeremiah, Wayne is Timothy, Elaine is a Martha..." When they came to Donnie they changed the pattern. They said they couldn't think of a biblical person's name, but felt her name should be "Peace." I might add that the girl that came to see Donnie was not part of the group that shared these names and had had no contact with them on this subject.

When they came around to me, they got really creative. They could only come up with "David." Not much revelation there, except that they said my passage was Psalm 18. I have to admit that I wasn't too impressed with that either, especially as, later, I began to read through the psalm. I didn't believe it applied to me at all until I got to verse 16: "He reached down from on high and took hold of me; he drew me out of deep waters."

Remember those four prophetic words about our ministry in Centerville? The third one was a vision of God reaching down, embracing me, and lifting me out of deep water. Hallelujah!

Chapter 13

THERE'S REVELATION AND THEN THERE'S REVELATION

R EVELATION? PROPHECY? GOD speaking through visions and dreams? What ever happened to the Reformation principle of *sola scriptura*—the Scriptures alone?

During the years of examining the Charismatic Renewal before evangelist Herb Mjorud laid his hands upon me in that school "upper room" auditorium in 1964 and for many years after that, the gift and teaching of the Renewal that I was the most skeptical about was the idea that God spoke today through visions, dreams, and the gift of prophecy.

It bothered me when someone would speak out during a meeting and say something like, "Thus sayeth the Lord: 'Yea, verily, with one accord thou shalt…'" as if God spoke in King James English or spoke at all outside of the Scriptures. I was even uncomfortable when teachers would say that prayer is not only talking, but also listening. The only two-way conversation with God I was used to was my talking to Him and Him speaking to me through the Scriptures.

The root of this block in my mind and spirit was at first cultural. I had always been taught that only schizophrenics hear from God, and my seminary training was even more convincing. It was completely hostile to the possibility of even a "still small voice," much less visions, dreams, and prophecy. For instance, our Lutheran Confessions, particularly the Smalcald Articles, say the following:

> In these matters, which concern the external, spoken Word, we must hold firmly to the conviction that God gives no one his Spirit or grace except through or with the external Word which comes before. Thus we shall be protected from the enthusiasts—that is, from the spiritualists who boast that they possess the Spirit without and before the Word and who therefore judge, interpret, and twist the Scriptures or spoken Word according to their good pleasure.[1]

I remember the dire warnings and words of condemnation concerning the "enthusiasts" (*Schwarmerei* in German). Was I an enthusiast? Would Luther condemn me if I heard from God? Even more frightening (after all, Luther was dead), would the LCMS condemn me? I remember the dread that filled my heart at the conference at Don Pfotenhauer's church in the Minneapolis area when during a time of questioning Dr. Ralph Bohlmann, an observer from the St. Louis Seminary, asked, "What is different in today's Charismatic movement from the enthusiasts that our Confessions so clearly condemn?" I don't remember who answered what, but I do remember believing that was and still is the sixty-four thousand-dollar question.

Even more convicting were the words on the next page in the Confessions mentioned above:

Accordingly we should and must constantly maintain that God will not deal with us except through his external Word and sacrament. Whatever is attributed to the Spirit apart from such Word and sacrament is of the devil.[2]

I believe that most everyone in the LCMS, especially the theologians who read those words, including myself, understood them to mean that all current revelation, such as visions, dreams, words of prophecy, or discernment of spirits are contrary to the Reformation's "Scripture alone" principle. It is interpreted as saying that God spoke that way in Bible times, but today He speaks through the Scriptures alone. All my life I believed exactly that until I discovered from the Scriptures themselves, from the Lutheran Confessions, and from personal experience that this great Reformation principle, *sola scriptura* (Scripture alone) did not, in effect, silence God after the first century.

I and all those I know in Lutheran Renewal firmly believe in the Reformation principle of Scripture alone. We are convinced that the Word and the sacraments are all we need, but we do not believe that the Confessions prohibit all other revelation from God and call it enthusiasm. As I said, I came to that conclusion from the Confessions themselves. For instance, the second section from the Smalcald Articles quoted above says just the opposite of what we all have believed. After saying "Whatever is attributed to the Spirit apart from such Word and Sacrament is of the devil," Luther goes on to say:

For even to Moses God wished to appear first through the burning bush and the spoken word, and no prophet, whether Elijah or Elisha, received the Spirit without the Ten Commandments. John the Baptist was not conceived without the preceding word of Gabriel, nor did he leap in his mother's womb until Mary spoke. St. Peter says that when the prophets spoke, they did not prophesy by the impulse of man, but were moved by the Holy Spirit, yet as holy men of God. But without the external Word they were not holy, and the Holy Spirit would not have moved them to speak while they were still unholy. They were holy, St. Peter says, because the Holy Spirit spoke through them.[3]

It seems clear to me that Luther is saying here that in the matter of revelation, God did not deal with the first century church, or even the Old Testament believers, differently than He deals with us today. He applied the same criteria concerning revelation in Bible times as He applies today. Luther's examples indicate this. Moses, the prophets, including Elijah and Elisha, and John the Baptist all needed an external word to make them holy. Once they received that external word, once they knew the Lord and were thus set apart (holy) for His service, then God revealed much to them. He spoke to and through them by the Holy Spirit. Luther is saying, however, that divine revelation is never direct or immediate.

Lutheran theology holds that revelation from God can be given to believers; the Holy Spirit can and does guide us. At the time of the Reformation there were individuals who went off the deep end, prophesying and sharing revelations that were out of harmony with the Bible. The Spirit works through the Word of God and makes us "holy" (believers, washed in the blood). That word is external, not "direct or immediate." First comes a knowledge of God through the Word, then personal guidance, not vice versa. Even the authors of the Scriptures had a preceding, external Word.

Paul said the same thing. He knew that everything is ours through the Word. He asked the Galatians: "Did you receive the Spirit by observing the law, or by believing what you heard?....Does God give you his Spirit and work miracles among you because you observe the law, or because you believe that you heard?" (Gal. 3:2, 5). He knew that we have all things in Christ, but that did not keep him from encouraging, commanding, and exhorting the believers to seek more of the Lord's work in their lives and more of the Spirit's gifts. This especially includes the revelatory ones that were not direct or immediate (then or now), but flowed from the Spirit through the preceding Word.

Lutheran theology is not dispensational, that is, it does not believe or teach that God deals with people differently at different times in history. There is a clear demarcation between the Old and New Testaments, but that separation is primarily the difference between before and after the coming of Jesus. Before was a time of waiting, longing, and prophetic hope. The New Testament era that came after is marked by the fulfillment of and involvement in God's plan for the salvation of the world that was foretold in the Old Testament era. In the past, the Holy Spirit was given only to select leaders. Now, the promise of His fullness is for all believers. (See Acts 2:17.) However, in both of these eras there is a unity at the core. They both center on Jesus Christ and the grace that saves based on His finished work.

In Lutheran theology, and I believe also in Scripture, the New Testament era consists of the last days, which extend from Jesus' first coming to His second coming and the end of the world. However, something unique did happen in the early church. God gave the church the inspired, infallible New Testament Word of God, "the faith which was once for all entrusted to the saints" (Jude 3). He does not reveal any new doctrines. That's been done "once for all." But God also gave the early church other revelations which did not establish doctrine, but were for guidance and direction, for encouragement and consolation (1 Cor. 14:3). These revelations were not infallible, but imperfect. They needed to be tested, submitted, and confirmed. (See 1 Corinthians 14:29, 1 Thessalonians 5:20–21, and 1 John 4:1.) The Scriptures themselves indicate that these revelations for local guidance and encouragement were expected to continue until the return of Christ when "the perfect comes" (1 Cor. 13:8–12). (See Acts 2:16–21 and 1 Corinthians 1:7–8.) That's the kind of revelation that, through the means of grace, is happening all over the world today in the renewal of the Holy Spirit. These people are not "enthusiasts," denying the written Word of God or twisting it to fit their "good pleasure."[4] (That's how they are described in the Lutheran Confessions.) Almost without exception, these believers are submitting themselves to the standard of the Word of God and the body of Christ, and through the power of the Holy Spirit and His gifts, they are building the kingdom of God as never before. Eighty to ninety percent of those coming to know Christ around the world are charismatic believers brought to faith through charismatic people.

Luther says in his Large Catechism (also one of our foundational Lutheran Confessions) that "Baptism promises and brings...victory over death and the devil, forgiveness of sin, God's grace, the entire Christ, and the Holy Spirit with His gifts."[5] For the non-Lutheran reader, let me assure you that we do not believe baptism is magic. Baptism is the "visible Gospel." That is, it is the good news of Christ Jesus proclaimed in a concrete, felt way. As the water is applied with the Word of God, it is telling the seeker that God loves them. He sent Jesus, His Son, to die for them that they might be forgiven and become children of God. Baptism is not effective without faith for "without faith it is impossible to please God" (Heb. 11:6). Faith is the hand that reaches out and receives all that grace offers. Faith receives Jesus. (See John 1:12.) And when you have Jesus, you have everything. It is in that sense that, just as the Word saves us by bringing us to Christ (James 1:21), so also "Baptism...now saves [us]" (1 Peter 3:21). It is in that sense that, as Luther said, "baptism promises and brings" all the things mentioned above.

I know that is true. The means of grace bring us to Jesus and Jesus to us, and when we have Him, we have everything. That being said, neither the Scriptures nor the church has ever interpreted that to mean that one should not desire the fullness of the Holy Spirit, nor that one should not desire the gifts of the Holy Spirit. He does not say, "Don't pray for the Spirit because you have Him too. In fact, don't hunger and thirst after anything. You have everything in the objective, external word and/or your baptism. You are filled with the Holy Spirit." Rather he says in 1 Corinthians 14:1, "Make love your aim, and earnestly desire the spiritual gifts, especially that you may prophesy" (RSV). In Ephesians 5:18 he says, "Do not get drunk on wine, which leads to debauchery. Instead, be filled with the Spirit." Paul tells the Romans that he longs to see them so that he can offer them spiritual gifts to strengthen them, implying that, in spite of their baptism, there is still the possibility of greater revelation. (See Romans 1:11.)

The writers of the Confessions were actually friends to Charismatic renewal. They knew that the Spirit works the same in all history since the Cross. They believed and said He gave gifts in their day, for they report that a contemporary Franciscan named John Hilten "predicted many things. Some of them have already happened, and others seem to be impending."[6] In another part of the text, they tell of a monk named Anthony who, when he "asked God to show him what progress he was making in his way of life, God pointed in a dream to a certain shoemaker."[7]

In other writings, Luther was especially clear that he believed the miraculous gifts of Mark 16 and 1 Corinthians 12 were not restricted to the "apostolic age" but were for his day also:

> These signs should be interpreted as applying to every individual Christian, when a person is a Christian he has faith and he shall also have the power to do these signs.[8]

> After the Word of the Gospel has been preached and the voice of rejoicing has sounded forth, there follows

the discernment of spirits and the distribution of the gifts of the Spirit of which 1 Corinthians 12:4 speaks.[9]

I especially like the following quotation:

> If the Holy Spirit would come in the course of such thoughts [methodical preparation for worshipful prayer]...and begins to preach in your heart with rich, illumined thoughts, do him the honor, let these rationally formulated thoughts, reflections and meditations fade away. Be still and listen for he [the Holy Spirit] knows better than you. And what he preaches note that and write it down. In this way you will experience miracles.[10]

So there is revelation and then there is *revelation*. There's the "once-for-all" revelation of the Scripture which "entrusted to the saints" the Christian faith and all its doctrines (Jude 3). But there is also the indwelling Holy Spirit and His gifts, which do not bring new doctrine, but apply the truths of the faith to everyday situations and thus build up, encourage, and console.

The latter revelations need to be tested by comparing them to the Holy Scriptures. The revelation and the Word must be in harmony. Other important questions to ask when testing a word of revelation include: Does the one who claims to be moved by the Spirit lift up Jesus as Savior and Lord? (See 1 John 4:1–3; John 15:26, 16:14; Revelation 19:10.) Is there fruit? (See Matthew 7:15–16.) Is there power to witness? (See Acts 1:8.) Is the ultimate result freedom? (See Romans 8:15; 2 Corinthians 3:17.)

The tests themselves are an indication that genuine, revelatory spiritual gifts are able to occur beyond the days of the apostles. Otherwise, why would the tests be given? If, as some believe, God used only the apostles to give the Spirit and His gifts or perform miracles and that they died out after the apostolic age (because the Scriptures were written and no more gifts were needed), then there would be no need for any other tests. In that case, if the apostles did the giving, the gifts would be genuine. That would be the only test needed. The mention of these tests, as well as others in the Scriptures, demonstrate that the gifts, as church history amply demonstrates, lasted far beyond the apostolic age and have been manifested in every century up through our own day.

The existence of counterfeits in any age are, apart from contributing to the need for such tests, also an indication that there are genuine gifts. The devil is not so foolish that he would counterfeit something that doesn't exist. Someone has pointed out the folly of counterfeiting an eight-dollar bill.

Knowing that according to 1 Corinthians 12:27–28, God has placed gifted people in the church (and no time limit is mentioned), and knowing that the gifts of the Spirit are subjective in nature, the early church tested the spirits. That's how they determined their validity (not because they were given by an apostle). They also knew that the gifts were real and so they warned against resisting or quenching the Spirit. It is no different today. If those days were the last days certainly these days are. We are in the same era and we need to test the spirits and acknowledge the reality of the gifts that pass the test lest we be guilty of resisting what God is doing.

If you have a relationship with someone, the two of you

communicate. I talk to Jesus and he talks to me. The devil talks to me too. He puts all sorts of temptations into my mind. I'm glad I can talk to Jesus about them and find in Him and in His word the strength to overcome. It has become incongruous to me that it's theologically all right with some if the devil talks to you, but not if you are hearing from Jesus.

The Scriptural and Confessional quotations, applications, and conclusions cited in this chapter were not part of my theological vocabulary when I first arrived at Centerville. My understanding has developed over years of wrestling with the whole issue of renewal in the Holy Spirit. And even after these fifty-plus years of study, my theology of the Spirit is still not cast in stone. I am open to learning much more about His ways. Emil Brunner said years ago in the third volume of his *Dogmatics:*

> The Holy Ghost has always been more or less the stepchild of theology and the dynamism of the Spirit a bug-bear for theologians....Theology through its unconscious intellectualism has often proved a significant restrictive influence, stifling the operations of the Holy Ghost, or at least their full creative manifestations....The miracle power of Pentecost, and all that is included under the concept of the charismata—the gift of the Spirit—must not be soft-pedaled from motives of a theological Puritanism.[11]

It may be true that all our efforts to interpret and theologize the dynamic, supra-logical workings of the Holy Spirit are doomed to imperfect propositions and conclusions at best. Only a legalist or a very myopic theologian would believe that the ultimate, essential goal of the workings of the Spirit is that we fit His mysterious ways into the framework of our systematic theology. Surely we must try to understand and formulate, but above all, we should be open to Him without fear. The Father does not give stones or scorpions. Surely we should try to reason things out and put them in some kind of order, but more importantly we should be open to one another and accept one another in Christ Jesus no matter how we may seek to explain the workings of the Holy Spirit in our lives. It was Jesus who likened Him to the wind. (See John 3:8.) One cannot box in the Holy Spirit, for "where the Spirit of the Lord is, there is freedom" (2 Cor. 3:17).

But it wasn't freedom that seemed to be on the horizon in Centerville. Most if not all of the theologians at the college agreed with that "blue Bible" sermon I had preached years earlier, declaring that tongues were little more than gibberish and miraculous gifts had expired. A storm was brewing.

Chapter 14

PRAYER AND THE MEANS OF GRACE

Y EARS AGO AS I was fellowshipping with other believers, probably at one of our pastoral conferences, one whom I considered to be a very experienced and wise pastor asked the question, "Do you know what makes the Missouri Synod unique among Christian denominations?" We all had our ideas, but his answer was, "Our 'means of grace' theology. No other denomination believes as we do." I remember that his statement struck me and instilled in me a certain pride that we were so unique. I now wonder if it shouldn't have rather alarmed me since the LCMS's current teaching on the means of grace seems to cause us to clash with other Scriptural truths, such as what the Bible teaches about prayer.

Historically a mark of any revival or renewal has been an increase in the appreciation and practice of prayer. In my experience, that has certainly been true of the Charismatic Renewal. If it has been anything, it has been a prayer movement. Although our meetings majored in praise and worship and there was always a sharing of the Word of God by one or more of those who attended, we called them prayer meetings because we all had come to a new experience and appreciation of the gift of prayer.

Prayer became much more to us than what the pastor read from a book of prayers on Sunday morning. It was suddenly communion with our Abba ("Daddy") Father. It was not a formal, memorized jingle you recited before and after meals. It was personal, intimate conversation with our best friend, a mountaintop experience of adoration and praise to the Savior of our souls and the Lord of the universe. It was the expression of the hand of faith that reached out and laid hold of the promises of God. It was the gift of a prayer language through which, when we ran out of words to describe the greatness, magnificence, and beauty of our God, the Spirit helped us—and we were edified. (See 1 Corinthians 14:4.)

St. Paul's teaching that tongues edify (spiritually build up) the individual underscores the problem that the reality of prayer poses to the LCMS's present 'means of grace' theology. The LCMS has a hard time harmonizing what Scripture and Luther say about prayer with that theology. There's a befuddling inconsistency in what is said about prayers on the one hand and, on the other hand, the insistence that God only acts through the means of grace. These are defined in the Lutheran tradition as the Word, the sacraments of baptism and the Lord's Supper, and possibly absolution (the announcement of the forgiveness of sins). For instance, Lutherans are proud to quote Luther as he indicates that he had so much to do on a given day that he didn't see how he could get it all done without at least three hours of prayer. Apparently Luther felt that prayer really made a difference. It moved God's hand. It brought measurable results from the Father who, in answer to prayer, intervened in his life to help get his work done. It isn't just psychological mind games. God really acts in the circumstances of time and space to change things in answer to prayer. In other words, prayer and its results are miraculous!

However, Luther says in the Confessions that "We should and must constantly maintain that God will not deal with us except through His external Word and sacrament. Whatever is attributed to the Spirit apart from such Word and sacrament is of the devil."[1] That statement, when quoted and understood out of context, is at the root of the muddled thinking concerning prayer. For instance, I remember talking about prayer with a good pastor friend who later became a staff person in one of the districts of the LCMS. He told me that he was pretty much convinced that praying for missionaries didn't do the missionaries any good. The benefits from such prayer were psychological, affecting the ones who prayed. It helped them set priorities, focus on what God wanted them to do, give more to missions, etc. In other words, my friend believed that prayer didn't move God to do anything. There are two reasons that explain how a Lutheran today might come to believe that:

1. We are all affected by our culture, which looks upon the miraculous as spooky at best.

2. Our Confessions seem to exclude prayer from being efficacious because they at face value indicate that the only way God acts (deals with us) is through His external Word and sacrament.

When I shared what was happening at our prayer meetings with a good friend and neighbor that served as a professor at the college in Centerville, he responded in much the same way as the pastor friend I just mentioned. He said, "Dave, when you tell troubled people to pray, you throw them back upon their own resources." He then went on to point out that one should direct them to the Word of God. In retrospect, I wish I would have had the foresight to say, "You're right, I should direct them to the Word, like Psalm 50:15—'Call upon me in the day of trouble; I will deliver you, and you will honor me'—and *then* pray with them."

The Word of God has the answer to every human need. A good Christian pastor, counselor, or teacher will use the Scriptures to bring wisdom and insight to bear on the difficulties and problems of life. But the ultimate answer and source of truth and life is not information. It is a person, the Lord Jesus Christ. Surely, He is present in the Word and sacrament. But He doesn't leave when we close the book or digest the bread and the wine. His life and truth are with us, and He answers when we call.

During this time, I noticed that LCMS publications were saying that prayer is not a means of grace. A few years later, some of the young men who had been in our home meetings had gone on to attend our two seminaries. When it became known that they claimed to have experienced a renewal in their lives from the Holy Spirit, including some of the gifts of the Spirit described in 1 Corinthians 12, they began to meet with opposition from the seminary administration. They were contacted and questioned about their experiences.

The young men shared how God had touched them. They

said that before their personal Pentecost they believed in Jesus as their Savior, were regular in church attendance, and had purposely gone to a Lutheran College to prepare for full-time ministry—but now their conviction was even more so! Their love for and commitment to Jesus was deeper. The Scriptures had become even more alive to them, and they were reading and studying them more regularly. Worship had become more exciting and was spilling over from Sunday morning into praises and thanksgivings throughout each day. They reported having new power to witness to their faith in Christ. God was doing today what He did in the early church.

You would think that there would be great joy at the seminary over what God had done in the lives of these new students. After all if what they were sharing were true, what greater goals could be desired for their students? But apparently some members of the administration were more concerned about the *means* than the end result. The ancient mix-up reared its ugly head again.

The students reported to us that some professors did rejoice with them. Nonetheless, the school authorities continued to make the twin errors, not necessarily taught, but caught by thousands of LCMS members: salvation by purity of doctrine (making ends out of means—see chapter 16) and the Synod's current interpretation of the "means of grace," the latter error being primarily a misunderstanding of the Confessions. As defenders of the faith and those called to oversee the indoctrination of future pastors, the administration responded to the students' testimonies by inaugurating a thorough program of investigation, persuasion, and ultimately purging of the Synod's seminaries.

You can imagine how difficult it was for these young men. They were novices seeking to defend themselves and their experiences before powerful authorities of their church, who they were conscience-bound to honor, respect, and obey. I'm sure these professors were sincere in their dealings with these young men. However, we did hear some stories of what I would term legalism and scholastic snobbery. I believe that sometimes these well-meaning professors were so blinded by their "superior" knowledge and positions that they were unable to really listen to these young men or open their minds to the possibility that what they were sharing was really true.

For instance, at least one professor, when told by students how edifying it was to pray and praise God with the gift of tongues, questioned, "Oh, you believe that the gift of tongues is a means of grace?" "Well, no, I wouldn't say that," the students responded. "St. Paul says that 'He who speaks in a tongue edifies himself,' and I've found that to be true" (1 Cor. 14:4). The professor then pressed the students, pointing out that the Confessions indicate that "prayer is not a means of grace and if, as you say, the gift of tongues is a prayer language, then how could it edify you when it is clear that the only way God has determined to deal with us is through the means of grace?" Of course, the students felt trapped and, in some cases, began to wonder if his experience was just emotional and whether he had perhaps been deceived. Some of these young men graduated and received calls to serve in LCMS congregations, but at great expense. The Spirit was quenched and they, in effect, denied their spiritual past.

Others, although they were overmatched as they tried

to debate their positions with these learned men, did not deny what they knew had happened to them in their spirits. They either left the seminary or, if they stayed, they were not given a call to an LCMS parish after graduation. I've followed what became of some of them, and they are serving the Lord mightily in other denominational or non-denominational congregations and/or missions and, through their ministry, the Holy Spirit is saving many souls for the kingdom. What is true of these seminarians is also true of the thousands and thousands of laypeople who have left the LCMS to serve God elsewhere: it is the LCMS's loss.

In the last chapter, I pointed out how the Confessions themselves (as well as Scripture) clearly indicate that the statement, "God will not deal with us except through His external Word and sacrament," is taken out of context and misinterpreted when it is understood to mean that the only time God speaks to us are those instances when we are at the table of the Lord or are reading, studying or remembering His Word. However, that seems to be exactly what most theologians and pastors understand that passage to mean. I say "seems to be" because it has been almost impossible to get a straight answer from them. In the mid 1980s, a number of the Renewal in Missouri (RIM) pastors met with key LCMS leaders, including the president of Synod, the chairman of the Commission on Theology and Church Relations (CTCR), and various seminary professors and district presidents, to discuss any theological differences RIM might have from official LCMS theology. At these dialogues, I asked more than once what that quotation meant. I could not get a straight answer.

The truth is that the Confessions do not limit the number

of sacraments. In the Apology of the Augsburg Confession, the writer says,

> Ultimately, if we should list as sacraments all the things that have God's command and a promise added to them, then why not prayer, which can most truly be called a sacrament? It has both the command of God and many promises. If it were placed among the sacraments and thus given, so to speak, a more exalted position, this would move men to pray. Alms could be listed here, as well as afflictions, which in themselves are signs to which God has added promises. But let us pass over all this. No intelligent person will quibble about the number of sacraments or the terminology, so long as those things are kept which have God's command and promises.[2]

Whether one says that prayer is or is not a means of grace, I believe prayer is more than that. It is a *goal* of the means of grace. The Word of God is the means through which the Holy Spirit creates faith in our hearts to come to God. Prayer (including the gift of tongues, the prayer language) is being with God. The Word and sacrament are the vehicles through which God comes to us. Prayer is the practice of His presence. The salvation of our God comes to us through the Word. In prayer we experience the goal and central reality of that salvation, communion with God.

The Word brings us the magnificent, manifold promises of God. Intercessory prayers and petitions verbalize the hand of faith to receive those promises. Scripture exhorts us to do this—verbalize our faith.

...call upon me in the day of trouble; I will deliver you, and you will honor me.

—Psalm 50:15

Ask and it will be given you; seek, and you will find; knock and the door will be opened to you. For everyone who asks receives; he who seeks finds; and to him who knocks, the door will be opened....If you then, though you are evil, know how to give good gifts to your children, how much more will your Father in heaven give the Holy Spirit to those who ask him!

—Luke 11:9–10, 13

The Word even tells us that at least one of the reasons we don't receive the blessings of the promises of God is that we don't ask. (See James 4:2.) How the LCMS has short-changed itself with its misunderstanding of the theology of the "means of grace." Cowed by misreading Luther's statement on how God deals with us, we have made the focus of our lives the pipe rather than the Living Water itself, the road rather than the destination, the plate rather than the bread, and the delivery system rather than the life.

When God is your focus, source, and goal; when you've drunk deeply of the Living Water and the promised rivers are flowing from your inmost being (see John 7:37–38); when you have tasted the Bread of Life and seen that God is good; when the Spirit of Christ who has promised to never leave you has filled you with His presence, then you may live a life of worship and praise, no matter what the circumstances. Like the lady who had a sign over her kitchen sink that said "Divine worship services held here three times daily," any activity can become an act of worshipful service to the glory of God.

Surely one needs to continue in God's Word (see John 8:31), but it is not a shortcutting of the "means of grace" or a flight from the Scriptures to find that growth in Christ comes in every situation of life. And for the one who trusts Him, God is present in every situation of life. Giant leaps of growth in Christ can and do happen when we are elsewhere from the Lord's table or His Word. That statement is not anti-"means of grace." Rather, it expresses the power of them.

Chapter 15

LET'S STUDY
THE BIBLE

W HEN OUR SENIOR pastor accepted a call to another congregation, we were saddened to see him go. He had become a dear friend and we worked well together. After his departure, my family and I missed him and his wife greatly. We had also become friends with many of the college professors and their wives and families. The administration and faculty of the college were very encouraging and were some of the best members of St. Mark's. With the other pastor leaving, I was left as the only called clergyman on the staff of this large congregation. The college's support did not wane as news of the charismatic prayer meetings held in our home spread around the campus and the town. However, there were a lot of questions being raised. The first and primary question in any such situation in the LCMS was theological. Was any false doctrine being taught? Is what was happening Lutheran? To deal with some of these issues, meetings were scheduled with about twenty-five faculty theologians.

One of the verifying aspects of the Renewal was how completely biblical it was at its core. The Bible's promises that Jesus would "baptize you in the Holy Spirit" and the references to the manifestations and gifts of the Spirit in the book of Acts and 1 Corinthians 12–14 were mysterious and puzzling to me before I experienced them. Besides believing that the miraculous gifts had disappeared forever, I had some crazy notions about them. But when they became a part of my life, I discovered how the passages made great sense. They fit. What the Bible says about them as they occurred long ago and far away in a completely foreign, Eastern culture is how I would describe them today from personal experience.

As I met with the theologians, my fears were confirmed to find that they had the same unfounded opinions about the Spirit and His gifts that I had once held. Our first area of disagreement concerned the nature of prophecy, the gift St. Paul especially promotes in 1 Corinthians 14. We were all in agreement that prophecy was not so much foretelling the future as it was "forth-telling," that is, proclaiming the Word of God. Because proclaiming the Word of God is what Christian preachers do, these theologians logically deduced that Paul was simply talking about preaching. It makes sense for Western Lutherans to believe this about prophecy because it solves both the cultural and the confessional problems that arise in applying the New Testament church life, doctrine, and practice to the present day.

From a cultural standpoint, the whole business of understanding the manifestations of the Spirit in Acts and the description of the gifts in 1 Corinthians 12 is scary. Reading about them is like watching a sci-fi movie. To our culture those manifestations and gifts are weird at best, but everybody knows what preaching is. That experience may be boring, but it isn't scary.

From the standpoint of the Confessions, all this confirms the conviction that the "Scripture alone" principle means what most in the Synod believe: that there is no divine revelation anymore other than that which is contained in Scripture. The preacher may believe he is inspired at times, but he understands that it comes from his careful study of the Word and his faithful proclamation of it.

During our meeting, I shared a number of points on the topic of revelation. A passage from O. S. Rankin in Alan Richardson's *A Theological Word Book of the Bible* says that the verb *propheteuein* ("to prophesy") is used three ways in the New Testament: to announce as a revelation from God, to reveal that of which the evidence has been hidden, and to foretell the future.[1] Just three years before these meetings, the Synod's Commission on Theology and Church Relations published a study paper entitled "Theology of Fellowship." It says:

> A prophet is one who speaks for God or a deity; a divinely inspired revealer, interpreter, or spokesman.... The term prophet in Scripture seems not to be used of teachers in general, but of divinely commissioned teachers into whose mouth God has put his Word and commanded them to proclaim it.[2]

The list in Ephesians 4:11 of ministry callings given by Jesus include apostles, prophets, evangelists, pastors, and teachers. This list and others in the New Testament indicate that the prophetic ministry was separate from that of preachers (pastors and teachers). Rankin also points out that it is hard to separate prediction from prophecy. Deuteronomy 18:22 and

Jeremiah 28:9 indicate that a true prophet can be identified by the fact that his predictions come true. This aspect of prophecy, although it is not of its essence, does give support to the idea that prophecy is not the result of the study and explanation of an already written revelation (the Scriptures), but it is rather a supernatural word from God. What else could prediction of future events be?

What Scripture reveals about the ministry of the prophet would support the idea that prophecy is divine revelation and not what we today think of as preaching. In Bible times there were many teachers and what today we would term *preachers* who proclaimed the Word of God, but they were not considered prophets. A prophet was someone special. The chief priests and elders of the people did not dare to speak against John the Baptist because they were "Afraid of the multitude, for all hold that [he] was a prophet" (Matthew 21:26, RSV). They were afraid to arrest Jesus for the same reason. (See Matthew 21:46 and Luke 7:16.) A prophet is able to discern by miraculous inspiration of God that which he could know no other way. When Jesus was blindfolded after His trial, the soldiers slapped Him and said, "Prophesy to us, Christ! Who hit you?" (Matthew 26:68). (See also Luke 7:39 and John 4:19.)

Gerhard Kittel's *Theologisches Wörterbuch Zum Neuen Testament, Vol. VI*, has this to say about prophecy, primarily based on 1 Corinthians 12 through 14:

> The primitive Christian prophet is a man of full self-awareness. When he is speaking he can break off if a revelation is given to someone else. When two or three prophets have spoken in the congregation others may

remain silent even though something is revealed to them (1 Cor. 14:29ff). They cannot influence the revelation itself. This comes from God with no cooperation on their part.[3]

All prophecy rests on revelation (1 Cor. 14:30). The prophet does not declare what he has taken from tradition or what he has thought up himself. He declares what has been revealed to him.[4]

...Prophecy is not the same as teaching [or preaching]. Whereas teachers expound the Scripture, cherish the tradition about Jesus and explain the fundamentals of the catechism, the prophets...speak to the congregation on the basis of revelation. Didaskalia [teaching] is instruction, propheteia [prophecy] deals with specific situations.[5]

For those who want to make a strict distinction between clergy and laypeople, as those in today's LCMS are want to do, it would also seem from 1 Corinthians 14 that prophecy is not preaching, for it is a gift also for the layman. 1 Corinthians 14:31 says, "You all may prophesy in turn." Although the prophet held a special position in the early church, the gift of prophecy could apparently operate in any member of the congregation, including women (1 Corinthians 11:5; 14:5, 24, 31, 39; Acts 2:17–18).

Kittel also points out that in the New Testament teaching is general instruction in doctrine, whereas prophecy deals with specific revelation for specific situations. (See 1 Timothy 1:18, 4:14, and Acts 13:1–3.) The LCMS's own sainted Dr. Victor Bartling (one of my professors at Concordia

Seminary, St. Louis) said in his paper on Spirit baptism and prophetic utterance: "The chief function of the New Testament prophet was to convey divine 'revelations' (1 Corinthians 14:26, 30) of temporary significance which proclaimed to the church what it had to do in special circumstances."

I was pleased to discover that these men—whose academic degrees far exceeded mine and possessed a sophistication in theological matters that put this parish pastor to shame—nevertheless listened to me and, as I remember, agreed with my research (which just confirmed my experience). In fact, I believe today's renewal in the Spirit has changed LCMS understanding concerning the Spirit and His gifts. I don't hear anyone saying anymore that prophecy is preaching. St. Paul says the main leadership positions in the church include prophets (Eph. 4:11), and as we've seen in 1 Corinthians, he highly promotes an earnest seeking of the spiritual gifts, especially that believers might prophesy (1 Cor. 14:1). If prophecy is not preaching, but rather sharing revelations straight from the throne, and if as a denomination we have concluded that the New Testament era extends from the first to the second coming of Christ, then what's a church to do?

I believe the obvious answer to that question is to change its contemporary misconception of the "Scripture alone" principle. As I said in a previous chapter, this principle did not mean to Luther nor the other writers of the Confessions, nor to myriads of Lutheran and other theologians since then that God fails to speak to and guide His people today. We shouldn't come up with some way to explain away His workings in the New Testament, workings which have continued throughout church history and into our day.[6] We simply need to be open to His personal guidance and realize that all present day revelation needs to be tested, particularly by the standard of all revelation, the Holy Scriptures, and also by the wise counsel of the saints. Our old selfish nature can get into the most holy places and twist, turn, and misuse even God's guidance and Word.

The second area of conflict between Renewal and non-Renewal theology was in the nature of the gift of tongues. The prevailing view was that in the book of Acts it was for missionary work, and in Paul's first letter to the Corinthians it was of a different kind: an ecstatic utterance of overly excitable, immature believers who were disrupting the Corinthian worship. At best, clergy and laity alike looked upon this gift as the least of the gifts and, at worst, as a present day counterfeit of a gift that even Paul looked down upon and even argued against using (1 Corinthians 14).

To learn more about the nature of tongues, I turned not to the library and its many biblical helps, but simply to the Scriptures themselves. I had found them to be quite clear and understandable on this topic if you examine them objectively without our cultural bias against anything miraculous. Again, I don't have a transcript of the meetings with the college theologians, but I believe I shared a lot of the following with them:

I'm convinced that the nature of the tongues described in the book of Acts is not essentially any different from that of the tongues Paul speaks of in 1 Corinthians 12–14. There is no indication that anyone was ever converted by the preaching of the gospel in tongues. In Acts 2:11, the people say, "We hear them declaring the wonders of God in our own tongues [language]." How was this accomplished? Did the disciples realize that they suddenly knew a new language and therefore found someone in the crowd to speak this new language to? It would appear that they simply began speaking. It doesn't say to whom they were speaking, nor does it say that they even knew what they were saying.

I believe light can be thrown on what happened in Acts 2 by the record of what happened in Acts 10 at the conversion of Cornelius. In Acts 11:17, Peter says of that episode that "God gave them [Cornelius and his friends] the same gift as he gave us, who believed in the Lord Jesus Christ." What did the disciples observe Cornelius and his friends doing? "They heard them speaking in tongues and praising God" (Acts 10:46). They were extolling, magnifying, giving glory to God. As the psalmist often magnified and praised God by telling of His mighty works in words of praise, so apparently these new believers were doing in tongues.

The reaction on Pentecost to these tongues-speakers was varied. Many present did not find it edifying at all—they thought they were drunk (Acts 2:13). The scriptures do not record that anyone was converted by this display. It was not a missionary tool. The world at that time had a common language used for inter-cultural communication, Greek, and needed no gift of tongues for the purpose of mission work. The mission work was accomplished when Peter spoke up and delivered his sermon (Acts 2:14–41). He explained that the men speaking in tongues were not drunk, which indicates that there may have been a sizable group of onlookers that thought they were. He presented the gospel and three thousand were baptized into Christ!

I believe the description of tongues in Paul's letter to the Corinthians is in harmony with this description in Acts for the following reasons:

- The same Greek word translated "tongues" is used in both Acts 2:4 and 1 Corinthians 12–14: *glossais*. Neither *ecstasy* in the New English Bible, nor *unknown* in the King James Bible are in the original.

- The Corinthian tongues are apparently also real languages. The phrase "speaking in tongues," used repeatedly to refer to this event, means, simply, "speaking in languages." In his argument that in church they should speak in a tongue only if an interpretation is given, Paul says, "Undoubtedly there are all sorts of languages in the world, yet none of them is without meaning. If then I do not know the meaning of the language, I shall be a foreigner to the speaker and the speaker a foreigner to me" (1 Cor. 14:10–11). He thus surely implies that tongues are indeed languages. His statement in 1 Corinthians 13:1, "If I speak in the tongues [*glossais*] of men and of angels, but have not love, I am only a resounding gong or a clanging cymbal," would indicate that tongues are languages. Whether they are known or unknown languages of men or of angels, the communication is meaningful. In 1 Corinthians

14:2 Paul says "For one who speaks in a tongue does not speak to men but to God. Indeed, no one understands him; he utters mysteries with his spirit." It would be hard to imagine one's spirit praying nonsense to God or praising Him with meaningless gibberish. Further, tongues are to be interpreted (1 Cor. 14:5). If one were merely uttering sounds, there would be nothing to interpret. The Corinthian tongues were real, translatable languages.

- The Greek word *exstasis*, as has been mentioned, is never used to describe a speaker in tongues. He is always referred to as simply "speaking." On two occasions (documented in Acts 2:7, 11 and 9:21), *exstasis* is used to describe those who heard and is usually translated "amazed." The idea that a speaker in tongues goes off into religious ecstasy and loses all emotional control is contrary to Scripture and experience. Paul puts certain controls and limits on speaking in tongues in church. This would indicate that they are not ecstatic, for this would imply a trance-like state beyond the control of the individual. It is possible that a particularly emotional person might become ecstatic in the midst of this experience, but this is an individual reaction and not a function of the nature of the gift of tongues. (The young girls who became ecstatic when listening to Elvis perform did so of their own emotional state, not because it was the nature of his music to elicit that response.) Otherwise Paul would not put controls on the public use of the gift.

- There is one thing that is mentioned about the gift of tongues in 1 Corinthians that is not mentioned in Acts, namely that the speaker in tongues doesn't know what he is saying. He is praying to God in the spirit, speaking mysteries in the spirit, blessing in the spirit, giving thanks in the spirit. This does not seem to conflict with the description of tongues in Acts where they are used to magnify God while telling of His mighty works. Nowhere in Acts is there any indication that the tongue-speakers knew what they were saying. Only on Pentecost (Acts 2) is there an indication that some hearers (not speakers) understood. Apparently not all hearers understood, for the reaction of many was that the disciples were drunk. It wasn't that the nature of tongues in the two books was different. The audience was different. The experience during the Feast of Pentecost, recorded in Acts, was significant because the city was filled with people from all over the Mediterranean world and God chose to give their languages as gifts. What a sign!

The usual use of the gift of tongues, then, is as a prayer language with which to praise, magnify, thank, and worship God. This definition of the gift has repeatedly been demonstrated to be true of modern-day speaking in tongues not only in books and testimonies, but in the experiences of people I know personally. The earliest example of this that I recall was with a schoolmate of mine from the seminary, Reverend Irwin Prange. We were at the first meeting of LCMS charismatic pastors at Pastor Bob Heil's church in Missouri in the late sixties, and Reverend Prange shared how he had gotten involved in the Renewal. A few years earlier he had attended a charismatic meeting in New York. He wasn't too impressed and, in fact, was going to leave early when a lady near him began to quietly pray in tongues. He was amazed to hear her speaking a psalm in Latin. He knew the language, and he knew the psalm, so he asked her where she learned to speak in Latin. She said that she hadn't ever learned to speak in Latin. That night Pastor Prange went alone into the chancel of his church and received the fullness of the Holy Spirit and the gift of speaking in tongues. Ever since that time, he has used this and other gifts in his ministry to the glory of God.

Another friend of mine, a missionary connected with Children of Promise International, a mission agency with Lutheran Renewal roots, told me years ago that one of his desires was to hear someone on the mission field speak in tongues in English. It happened that he and his wife got into Venezuela and planted a church of new believers. After a furlough back in the United States, they wanted to go back to Venezuela, but the country had been closed to foreign missionaries and he couldn't get a visa. For years he tried, and then one day he was in a neighboring country at a prayer meeting. A native of that country spoke up in the meeting and said in clear and precise English that God was going to open the door to Venezuela and they would soon be able to return and continue the work there. They later discovered that this native did not speak or understand a single word of English.

In my mind the most humorous and meaningful example of tongues being the miraculous expression of a real language happened at, of all places, the most anti-Holy Spirit Renewal place in the synod: another Concordia Seminary (not my alma mater), which at the time was located in Springfield, Illinois (today it is located in Fort Wayne, Indiana). As part of their program of indoctrination against the Renewal, the seminary invited Dr. Paul A. Qualben, a psychiatrist from New York, to present a lecture to the student body on a study he had conducted concerning the Renewal. On the college staff that year was a visiting professor, the Reverend Risto Santala, who had recently been teaching in Israel. He heard the lecture and wrote a letter to Dr. Qualben which began (see Appendix I for a full copy of the letter):

> Less than two weeks ago you had a lecture about the phenomena of glossolalia.... Among the examples given, we heard also a tape where one and the same man spoke five different languages and sang a liturgical chant. According to the tape which I got of this lecture [you said that] "linguists that have analyzed many tapes of persons speaking in tongues have not found any of them representing a known language or dialect." Since I've been preaching and teaching more than ten years in modern Hebrew in Jerusalem and since I've been used to medieval RASHI-Hebrew and Talmudic texts, I felt that it would be good to notify you of the treasure which you have in your hands.[7]

Pastor Santala proceeded to give a detailed commentary on the music and text of this chant "treasure." He described it as a "hypodorian A-reciting tone, similar to Gregorian chant, though its roots are in pre-Gregorian monophonic plainsong." Reverend Santala went on to explain that "this type of singing traces back to the first Christian hymns and the ancient temple service." He further commented that "the song has all the signs of professional musical work." With respect to the text of the chant in tongues, he pointed out that it was based mainly on Numbers 6:24, "The LORD bless you." He indicated that "the holy name of God, which is never pronounced by a religious Jew, is however departed [in the chant] to two synonyms of God, *El* and *Jah*, theologically a very interesting solution."

After mentioning that he had been studying singing for about eight years with a well-known Jewish professor, Pastor Santala affirmed the authenticity of the pronunciation and singing style, saying, "I must admit that this man glides over the words very distinctly and smoothly." Then he offered a literal translation of the text:

> ... May the Lord bless thee O Man ... of His O Man of-Him-He bless the bride that God shakes you, He hears and blesses the bride. Behold He and He will bless completely as if in heaven in order to save and God reveals His full power. The light of Messiah becomes wonderful. He will answer, He saves. I shall bless the bride with strong latter rain, He hears raise (presumably corresponding [to] the Latin Sursum Corda).

"Its music and linguistic level is high, but the theological concepts are still deeper," writes Santala. He continues:

The Man addressed is a "Man of-Him-He." Some Jewish scholars, like the Swedish Chief Rabbi Gottlieb Klein, have stated that the forbidden name of God would be originally *Ani ho, Ani hu,* or in its Aramaic form, *Ana ho* or *Ana ko.* The original term translated "Man of-Him-He" is the best combination of this hidden name, An-da-ko-ho. He is a Man and He blesses the bride, the congregation. Even Luther tried to solve the mystery of this name in his book *Vom Schem Ha-Mephorasch.*

Santala commented repeatedly on the ancient authenticity of the chant and referenced many verses of scripture in support of and connection with its theology.

The most interesting prophecy in this song is the promise of "the latter rain".... According to our Hebrew Bible Joel 3:23 reads as follows: "He will give you the former rain for righteousness (or the 'teacher of righteousness' like in the Scrolls of the Dead Sea and in some Jewish rabbinic sources) and he will cause to come down for you the rain, the former rain and the latter rain." The former rain begins the rain season and the latter comes always just before the harvest forming the flesh for the grain—in accord to this many Christians believe that there will be a short time of blessing before the second Advent.

I was also especially impressed with the last part of that chant and its mention of the "latter rain." In both Old and New Testaments, the figure of rain and/or poured water is a figure of the giving of the Holy Spirit. To millions of people around the world, today's outpouring of the Holy Spirit (the latter rain, perhaps) has been a blessing and a most significant factor in multiplying the church today at a greater rate than at any other point in history—perhaps, as Reverend Santala said, just before the second advent.

Copies of Reverend Santala's letter were circulated through the seminary student body and faculty. This experience is not unusual. Many who have been involved for some time in the Renewal can share testimonies of those who have heard the gift of tongues spoken in a language they understood, and many more can share testimonies of the present reality of the operation of all gifts of the Spirit, such as healing and discernment, etc. Myriads of people have been won to Christ as these manifestations accompany the preaching of the gospel. But a mark of a pharisee is resistance to any kind of change, and it is not surprising that little notice was taken to the rich treasure Reverend Santala spoke of, though many read his letter. This resistance creates blindness to truth, even when it's right in front of your face.

What the Scriptures say about this strange gift of tongues and what people in our day are experiencing as they use this gift make a lot of sense to me. There are simply not enough words in any one language to give praise and glory to the beauty, majesty, and love of God. When one's heart is bursting with the joy and the love of Jesus, I have found it to be a real privilege to be able to praise Him in a language that He Himself supplies through His Spirit. But speaking in tongues can also be a gift for the church when the Spirit urges someone to speak out loud in tongues for the edification of the congregation. In this case, the speaking in tongues should have an interpretation so that all present can understand and enjoy what is being said. The experience of giving interpretations is similar to the experience of prophecy. The interpreter, like the speaker in tongues, does not understand the tongues. (See 1 Cor. 14:2, 14.) In other words, the gift of interpretation is not a gift of translation. It is an urging to speak words that are given.

One man tells of the following experience to illustrate this use of tongues:

> A few years ago this man went with a choir to a church to give a performance. Many of the choir members had become involved in the renewal of the Holy Spirit. During the concert, in a moment of silence, one of the choir members spoke in tongues and then another one gave the interpretation. The rest of the choir was embarrassed because they were afraid that the audience would not understand. But it turned out that right afterward, the pastor of the church turned to the choir director and asked her if she knew the men. When she replied that she did, he asked her if they knew Hebrew. When she replied that they did not, he told her that he knew Hebrew and that the first man had given a message in perfect high Hebrew and the second man had given an almost literal translation of the message. It was enough to convince the pastor of the validity of the gift of tongues.[8]

The discussions I had with the college professors were augmented by a Bible Study we began with the Board of Elders. They also had questions. People were talking. Some of it was negative, with charges of emotionalism and questions about the gift of tongues. But, thankfully, I believe at least partly because of these studies and discussions together, the furor died down and faith continued to grow across the campus.

Chapter 16

LET'S NOT STUDY
THE BIBLE

I T WAS ALMOST a year before we found another pastor
to fill out our staff at St Mark. We finally interviewed a
brother—I'll call him John Schmidt—who was serving a
church in the West, and he accepted our call. His title would
be administrative pastor and mine, simply pastor. Guidelines
were drawn up and passed by the voters that spelled out a
co-pastorate of brothers working together, making decisions
together, and sharing responsibility under the leadership
of the administrative pastor. He arrived early in the year.
I remember the excitement Donnie and I had as we drove
over to their home to welcome them as they were moving
in. It was a real relief to know that I wouldn't carry the load
alone anymore. We had talked together at length during his
visit with us before he accepted the call, and as I had with
the senior pastor before him, I shared with him my experiences with the Holy Spirit. Although he didn't agree with me,
he assured me that he felt it would be no problem working
together as co-pastors to build the kingdom. I was soon to
learn that was not the case at all.

Pastor Schmidt's first sermon to the congregation was

a message on pastor-people relationships. His next message was delivered to the congregation while I was helping take the youth on a weekend retreat. I returned from the retreat during the late service's sermon. Our offices were on the lower level but were wired for sound from the sanctuary. I could hear the message perfectly, and what pastor Schmidt was saying filled me with dread. My stomach churned as I listened to him mouth the same stuff I had said years earlier: that the miraculous, revelatory gifts of the Spirit ceased during the apostolic age and there was no such thing as being baptized in the Holy Spirit. I guess I should have expected it since I had been there myself. However, because we had talked about these issues and he had said that we could, in spite of our disagreements, work together, this sermon was totally unexpected. It hit me like a ton of bricks.

But God is faithful! A young neighbor of ours (she was a student at the college, but lived with her parents) named Gretchen did what the Bereans did: examined the Scriptures "to see if these things were so" (Acts 17:11, RSV). She also did some personal investigation, showing up at our next prayer and praise meeting. She soon became a regular participant and has since been faithfully serving the Lord as a wife, mother, teacher, and missionary in Hong Kong.

What I am about to recount now is the most difficult part of this story. This chapter and the next two tell of the last few months that led up to that dreadful voter's meeting. Just thinking about that experience again, even after more than thirty-five years, is stressful to me. But this story is not about my struggles and hurt. I don't want to be an "accuser of the brethren" (Rev. 12:10) as I write about these very difficult months in my life. I do not hold any bitterness or anger toward Pastor Schmidt or the Board of Elders. I understand where they were coming from. I can honestly say that I love them all as Christian brothers and look forward to being with them in heaven. I have no desire to justify myself or bring condemnation upon anyone. Our enemies are not people. We are not battling against people but "against the principalities, against the powers, against the world rulers of this present darkness, against the spiritual hosts of wickedness in the heavenly places" (Eph. 6:12, RSV). Consequently, my reason for sharing these things is solely to unmask the strategies of the enemy and to show the faithfulness of God in the midst of it all.

A legalist (of whom I was once a chief), just like the Pharisees Jesus encountered, can have a zeal for God that "is not based on knowledge" (Romans 10:2). The pharisaic zeal for the status quo of Jesus' time kept them from salvation. Even today, zeal without love could have the same result, but in my experience, it mainly is a cause for legalism and division in the one body of Christ. Today's pharisaic zeal can lead to doing things that are intended to serve the kingdom, but are unethical and devious. Rather than name any names or go into detail about who did what or repeat everything that happened, for the rest of this chapter I'm just going to list some things that happened and point out, again, the faithfulness of God in it all. The following experiences are not necessarily in chronological order.

We stopped studying the Bible in elders meetings. My continuing plea was, "let's study the Bible." I remember on one occasion bringing it up again privately to one individual and saying something like, "Let's get our Scriptures out and look at what they say about these things. That's all I'm asking." It's hard to believe, but the essence of the response was, "It wouldn't be fair. One who hasn't had the opportunity to study these Scriptures on the charismata like you have all these years would have no chance to win a discussion of these issues." In other words, the issue was not seeking out the truth or submitting to the Word of God, but winning a debate!

Years later at our bi-annual LCMS convention, a resolution was passed that required representatives from the synod, who were chosen by the synodical president, to meet with representatives from Renewal In Missouri (RIM) to discuss any differences that might exist between RIM and the synod. I was one of the RIM representatives. Papers were delivered from both groups. We had cordial and fruitful discussions on the issues. We found we agreed on almost everything, but we never just opened our Bibles and studied them together. Toward the end of the third of these productive retreats, one of the brothers from RIM suggested we all just study the Bible together. It never happened.

The legalistic spirit will tolerate obvious contradictions like trumpeting "Scripture alone," while remaining unwilling to study those same Scriptures if they would at all compromise the denominational party line. As I have tried to understand the positions I once held and as I see some of the younger men coming out of seminary with the legalistic training that is making a comeback in the synod, I have come to believe that purity of doctrine in all its parts seems to have been added to the gospel as a component of the way of salvation for the legalist! The reasoning seems to go like this: the whole

Bible is inspired by God and every doctrine in the Word of God is important (I agree with both of these assertions); the LCMS understanding of those doctrines is accurate and true (as an article of faith I agree, but with the understanding that we are all fallible and therefore our interpretation could be and probably is in certain areas, mistaken); anyone who does not believe exactly as we do is in error (a possibility), and it is a loving thing to expose error because it is dangerous to salvation to hold to it (it depends on the error).

What does this reasoning do to the commendation Jesus gives to child-like faith in Luke 18:17? A child may have some pretty wild ideas about eschatology, absolution, transubstantiation, asceticism, objective versus subjective justification, Docetism, kenoticism, or chiliasm, but if that child knows and trusts in Jesus as his or her Savior, he or she is a giant in the kingdom—greater than John the Baptist. Not knowing and therefore not believing all the doctrines does not diminish that child's value or position as a child of the King and my sister or brother in Him. The child's denomination also doesn't matter.

Instead of studying the Scriptures, elders meetings became forums to bring up concerns about the prayer meetings in our home and my involvement in the Charismatic movement. These concerns became charges. Then the charges were formulated into "guidelines," a nice term for the proposed prohibition of what Donnie and I firmly believed God was doing in our midst.

One of the first concerns that became a charge and then a guideline was the issue of unionism. Because Donnie and I had attended Full Gospel Business Men's Fellowship

International meetings and other churches where Renewal speakers were scheduled, we, said the charge, had committed unionism. (Unionism, as I pointed out in chapter seven, is that unique LCMS doctrine that says it is sinful to lead or have joint services with churches of denominations that are not in fellowship with the LCMS because their doctrines are in error). I pointed out that the Fellowship is not a church. Even if it were, it would not be unionism to attend another church or to pray with other Christians, even according to the LCMS's standards. Such things are—or should be— encouraged rather than discouraged. Although we felt it was a serious encroachment on our freedom in Christ Jesus, Donnie and I agreed not to attend any more Fellowship or other Renewal meetings until the issue was settled with the elders through a study of the Scriptures.

At about this time it began to appear that the congregation leadership was going to investigate the Scriptures! Pastor Schmidt and the elders scheduled a study group on the Charismatic movement for an upcoming Monday. It would include the board of elders and the staff of the church and parochial school. I asked that the theology department of the college be invited.

I'm not sure how it happened, but the two spring conferences for LCMS pastors in our area that year included major presentations on the Charismatic movement by professors from our St. Louis Seminary, and they were both scheduled just before our study group meeting. I had a suspicion that what was happening at Centerville was a major reason for the topics and scheduling of those presentations. Of course, the pastoral staff (Pastor Schmidt and myself) from St.

Mark's, along with a large contingent of the college theologians, attended the first gathering, held at a host church in a neighboring community in mid-May.

I was very nervous as Dr. Fred Danker, a New Testament Greek scholar, stood up to make his presentation. He was given an hour and a half, which began with the following story:

> Rabbi Jacob Rabinowitz was the descendant of seventy generations of rabbis, and he was a secret disciple of our Lord. Some years ago, he was invited to an Assemblies of God meeting in Pasadena, Texas. The preacher saw him kneeling there and he asked him what his special problem was. But the Jew could not answer. He was quite absorbed in the situation. The preacher had the charismatic gift of "sophia" [Greek for "wisdom"] and he told him, "Well, that's all right. God knows better than you what is lacking."
>
> Then he asked the congregation to pray for this man. Some of them came forward and laid their hands on the man's shoulders and on his head, and then they all prayed, some in English and some in strange tongues. All of a sudden the rabbi jumped up and asked who of them was a Jew. No one answered and he went on, "Who of you knows me? Forgive me if I don't recognize you."
>
> And still there was no answer. Then he said, "I heard it from that side...Yes, right where you are standing!" He asked the man he was pointing at, "Sir, are you a Jew?"
>
> The man said, "Uh, no. I'm Irish."
>
> "You have the accent. But where did you learn Hebrew?"
>
> "Well, I don't know any Hebrew," the man said.

"But you just spoke Hebrew," the Jew said. "And how do you know my name and the name of my father? You said, in perfect Hebrew, 'I dreamed a dream. Those who do not understand will understand you for you, Jacob, son of Ezekiel the rabbi, will come in the power of the gospel of Jesus Christ.'"[1]

Dr. Danker went on to say, "Now this is one of the very many documented recitals of the strange circumstances that have taken place...especially in the United States and then mushrooming from our country into all parts of the world. This movement...is called 'the Charismatic movement.'" Dr. Danker continued to speak favorably of the Renewal and encouraged the pastors to look into it. He described the early church's openness to the Spirit's gifts and their expression in their meetings as a source of their "extraordinary vitality," a vitality that was soon slowed down in the "mud of history." Later centuries determined that tongues and miracles were to get the early church started, but we can't expect them in our day. Danker continued:

> But at the time of the Reformation, there was to some extent a liberation from this oppressive pall of law and order in the name of religion. Luther blew the whistle on the tyranny of the intellect and of ecclesiastical politics as the central ingredient in Christianity.... Therefore the church must be especially alive to the fact that God may, in these latter days, be speaking to us through people who seem to come to us from the fringes of unorthodoxy and what we, in our arrogance and our social suavity, call "fringe-line sects." Where else is He going to pop out if He can't come

out through the mainline churches? Perhaps in these particular decades and even now, He is saying something to us from humble little places like Bethlehem or Nazareth instead of central headquarters, Jerusalem. In other words, if we're going to operate with the assumption that miracles have passed, then we are not going to understand the Charismatic movement, that is, if we're going to let our traditional rationalism prevail. And let's face it, we have been given over to all kinds of rationalistic procedures whereby we are able to manipulate God and exploit people in the name of religion. When we can formulate God and God's revelation's about Himself in such a way that we can handle these and then clobber one another while we are claiming to love and adore God, then we have put God in an untenable position and then God has to come and express Himself through people of other tongues. Therefore, the fact that the tongues movement has grown apace and has now even invaded the mainline churches, including the Lutheran churches, is indicative to me that God is speaking in these latter days to us who are....entrenched in mainline...orthodoxy."[2]

I loved it! "The oppressive pall of law and order in the name of religion" was a perfect description of legalism. The centrality of "the tyranny of the intellect and of ecclesiastical politics" and being "entrenched in mainline...orthodoxy."—sectarianism! "Our arrogance and social suavity"—spiritual pride! I believe Danker was right. All of these abominations have appeared in various forms and times in the LCMS tradition. And they were seeking again, at that time, to take control in our denomination.

There wasn't much that Dr. Danker said that could be used to discredit the Renewal so, of course, the pastoral staff and some of the professors went to the next conference. On May 20 in another community, Dr. E. V. Kalin, made his presentation. Again, I was nervous (I was a slow learner) as he stood up to speak.

Dr. Kalin's presentation was in three parts. The first offered the history of Pentecostalism. The next explained neo-Pentecostalism and how it came to be, and the last was an evaluation of the Charismatic movement. He also spoke most favorably of the Renewal. However, in part of his evaluation he pointed out that he disagreed with seeing the Christian life as "two distinct stages of experience," that is, conversion and a subsequent baptism of the Holy Spirit. Dr. Kalin felt, and the LCMS has traditionally taught, that there is only one experience—conversion. At the time that bothered me greatly because it seemed to conflict with Scripture and my own experience, but today I can see it being understood in that way. I believe that when we have Jesus, we have everything. He is the beginning and the end. The rest of the Christian life, a life of growing up into Christ and growing sanctification, is simply the appropriation of all that we have in Christ Jesus, which includes the fullness of the Holy Spirit and His gifts.

Someone said to me long ago that you can say anything in the LCMS if you just use the right words. If I had been able to express my experience in the right words, I think some things would have been different. But isn't that a shame? No matter how you express it, the reality is the same. Christianity is to be filled with the Spirit of God and zeal for His kingdom. If you can't explain that in orthodox words, so what? It is the New Testament reality that counts.

Immediately, a memo was sent out from the church office to the members of the May 24 study group on the Charismatic movement. A transcript of Dr. Kalin's remarks on the baptism of the Holy Spirit was included, along with the comment that "the introduction, which is not included, spoke of the history of the Charismatic movement." Recognizing this information to be erroneous, I submitted the following memo as a follow-up to the one distributed by the church office:

> What was left out of Kalin's paper was not the introduction as is stated in the letter announcing the agenda of the meeting. What was left out was the first two and a half points of his presentation (out of three)! Professor Kalin spoke favorably about the Charismatic Renewal. In fairness to his wishes and position I feel we should at least take the first half of his evaluation as part of our agenda.
>
> Theological considerations are an issue.
>
> People are also an issue. "By your fruits you shall know them," says the Scripture—not by your exegesis, not by your correct theology. We are not only to examine the theology of the Charismatic movement, but also its fruits, what is happening.
>
> Therefore I propose that we invite some of those involved to speak on what has happened in their lives. People's lives are an issue. I know that Dr. Kalin is distressed [I had called him and told him what was happening] that only that part of the presentation that appears to be negative is discussed in our meeting. He is not negative to the Renewal. He personally said

to me: "I definitely believe that God is pouring out his gifts to the people involved in the Charismatic Renewal. I am one thousand percent in favor of the Charismatic Renewal."

I frankly don't remember much from that study meeting except that it once again wasn't really a Bible study, but rather the presentation of opinions. My memo was ignored, and all the information from the two conference speakers, with the exception of the one theological difference that seemed negative, was excluded. It was a big meeting: including the teachers, the church's staff numbered eighteen; the board of elders numbered twelve; and the department of theology, eleven. The district president and circuit counselor were also there. The attack continued.

The guidelines proposed by the elders concerned manifestations of the Spirit. One line put it this way: "All shall be cautious that the phenomena of speaking of tongues does not intrude into the public worship of the congregation."

In 1 Corinthians 14:26–29 and 39–40 Paul gives his guidelines for public worship:

> What then shall we say, brothers? When you come together, everyone has a hymn, or a word of instruction, a revelation, a tongue or an interpretation. All of these must be done for the strengthening of the church. If anyone speaks in a tongue, two—or at most three—should speak, one at a time, and someone must interpret. If there is no interpreter, the speaker should keep quiet in church and speak to himself and God. Two or three prophets should speak, and the others should weigh carefully what is said.... Therefore, my

brothers, be eager to prophesy, and do not forbid speaking in tongues. But everything should be done in a fitting and orderly way.

Paul's very clear directive to the church—"do not forbid speaking in tongues"—made in the context of its public gatherings for worship, is directly contradicted by the above guideline imposed by the elders. I didn't object because I knew that this particular guideline was built on a misconception concerning tongues, a misconception that a joint study of the Word would have cleared up. God doesn't overpower the speaker of tongues so that he has no control. Paul wouldn't have given directives to control the gifts if that were the case. I knew that none of the students would burst out in tongues in a public service at St. Mark's because they knew it would have been disruptive and counterproductive.

Sometime in the middle of the proclamation of the guidelines, it appeared that we were finally going to have a Bible study on the Renewal for the church members who were interested. A Bible class was scheduled for the 9:15 a.m. Sunday school hour to study the Charismatic movement! However, I soon learned that I would not be teaching it. The first session was scheduled on a day I would be helping lead a youth retreat and the next on a morning when I would be preaching during the 9:15 service!

Apparently some members also considered the arrangement to be unjust and interceded enough so that another session was scheduled which I could attend. It was to be the Sunday before these previously scheduled classes. Pastor Schmidt would teach during the first half hour of that class and I would take the second half hour to responding to what he had to say. That didn't sound too good to me for the following reasons:

As I mentioned earlier, one of the truths of God's Word that the Spirit ingrained in my heart through the Renewal is that God hates division in the body of Christ. There is one church and no matter what our differences if we trust in Jesus as our Savior, we are brothers and sisters. The scripture that should guide our attitudes toward and relationships with our brothers and sisters in Christ is Ephesians 4:1–6:

> I therefore, a prisoner for the Lord, beg you to lead a life worthy of the calling to which you have been called, with all lowliness and meekness, with patience, forbearing one another in love, eager to maintain the unity of the Spirit in the bond of peace. There is one body and one Spirit, just as you were called to the one hope that belongs to your call, one Lord, one faith, one baptism, one God and Father of us all, who is above all and through all and in all. (RSV)

Because of these convictions, I felt if I responded negatively to my brother pastor's presentation, it would not serve to keep the unity of the Spirit. I told him that I would be glad to meet with him alone or with the elders and talk about these issues as we studied the Scriptures together, but I believed it would be a mistake to have the two pastors debating each other in front of the sheep. This could only cause more division, which God hates.

The Sunday morning arrived for the great co-pastors' presentations. The fellowship hall was filled. Pastor Schmidt presented a paper in the first half hour, accompanied by charts and graphs and other visual aids. I was given to understand that the topic was going to be the gift of tongues, so I just presented my understanding of the biblical material relative to that gift. Pastor Schmidt offered closing remarks, in which he pointed out that the paper was not his but rather that of the Synod's CTCR.

Even though I was shocked, as were many others in attendance, I was also blessed. Leading up to our presentations, Pastor Schmidt had made repeated suggestions that I ready myself to refute the arguments he was prepared to make. If I had not been sensitive to the Spirit and had instead pointed out flaws in my co-pastor's presentation, I not only would have been disagreeing with Pastor Schmidt but also with the mother church, an unpardonable sin according to many in the denomination. There was still a lot of denominational pride and loyalty in those days. There was a conviction, especially among the older generation, that the LCMS was not a human institution—as all denominations are—but the one true church. What came from headquarters was virtually on a par with Scripture. But, God is faithful! I praise Him for once again guiding and strengthening me through His Word! (The paper Pastor Schmidt shared was a first draft of a subsequent study paper published by the CTCR. This first draft had contradictions and some pretty poor theology in it, but I kept my usually verbose mouth shut. Incidentally, the CTCR completely rewrote that study paper before it was published. Many on the commission were shocked to hear that it had been used before publication.)

For individuals focused on legalism, protecting the purity of the faith in all its parts is a holy mission that takes precedent over almost everything. The Lutheran Reformation was primarily about establishing the belief in justification (being made right with God) by God's grace through faith in Jesus Christ as Savior. That central truth is what Lutherans major in, and that's good, except that Lutheran theologians seem to have a kind of tunnel vision focused on justification alone. It's almost as if it joins faith, grace, and Scripture alone as a kind of fourth main tenet of the Reformation. All the rest of theology is interpreted in connection with justification and reacted to on the basis of that theology. Sanctification (Christian growth in good works) is considered a weak sister at best, yet the Charismatic Renewal is about sanctification.

For instance, for the Lutheran, the main thing about the Holy Spirit is that He brings us to faith. He, through Word and sacrament, creates faith in our hearts to trust the Lord and keeps us in that faith. That's about it as far as a LCMS emphasis on the Holy Spirit. From the standpoint of the average Lutheran, all this stuff about gifts and miracles and experiencing God is not only culturally weird, it's theologically suspect, because it's interpreted in terms of justification rather than sanctification. Another for instance: a "Charismatic movement discussion guide" that was used at one of the study groups addressed the topic, "The certainty and validity of a Christian's faith." It posed two apparently opposing statements regarding the nature of certainty in faith. It said that some strongly believe that one's faith "is dependent on, and verified by, personal experience." Others, says the guide, just as strongly believe that one's faith "is based on the objective message of the saving activity of God which culminates in the events of the life, death, resurrection and ascension of Jesus Christ." Well, any good Lutheran would know that the latter option is the true one. Of course, the implication is that Charismatics strongly believe—erroneously—the former and that the Renewal is about justification.

Through my godly parents who taught me the Scriptures, I knew who my Savior was and trusted Him totally for my salvation long before I became involved in the Renewal. In fact, I can't remember a time I didn't know and trust in Him, and I can even remember miraculous answers to prayer as a child. I'm convinced that this was also true of most if not all the young people that attended our prayer meetings. This does not, however, deny that God gives to faith based upon the Word, but wonderful experiences do verify the Word. Hebrews 2:3–4 says, "How shall we escape if we ignore such a great salvation? This salvation, which was first announced by the Lord, was confirmed to us by those who heard him. God also testified to it by signs, wonders and various miracles, and gifts of the Holy Spirit distributed according to his will." (See also Romans 15:18–19 and Mark 16:15–18.)

To scoffing unbelief and pharisaic opposition, Jesus said, "A wicked and adulterous generation asks for a miraculous sign" (Matt. 12:39). But to the faith of Peter's confession, "You are the Christ, the Son of the living God" (Matt. 16:16), Jesus gives a mountain-top experience as "he was transformed before them, and his face shone like the sun, and his garments became white as light" (Matt. 17:2, RSV). To those who said the source of His mighty deeds was Satan He said, "But if I drive out demons by the Spirit of God, then the kingdom of God has come upon you....anyone who speaks against the Holy Spirit will not be forgiven, either in this age or in the age to come" (Matt. 12:28, 32). Jesus was quite concerned when He did perform a miracle that it be received as a sign of the kingdom of God and not of Satan. I am sure He is just as concerned about the miracles He has worked through the church after Pentecost and up to this day. They all are meant to be signs of the kingdom, the presence of God, the King.

Another question asked in the discussion guide was, When you don't feel God is present, where do you turn?—To the Word of God or to personal experiences?

Another question asked: If one wants to be more dedicated, how does he receive this power for greater dedication?—Through Word and sacrament or through personal experiences?

Note how the objective Scriptures are juxtaposed in an adversarial position to subjective personal experiences, as if one was the enemy of the other. As we noted back in chapter 8, there is an anti-miracle bias in the LCMS (and, I believe, in many other denominations) that is not only cultural. It is unfortunately also theological, even in a church that prides itself on its faithfulness to the Bible, a book that is filled from cover to cover with experiences of the miraculous power and manifest presence of God.

Dr. Martin H. Franzmann, one of my favorite professors at Concordia Seminary in St. Louis wrote *Follow Me*, my favorite book on the Gospel of Matthew. In it he put his finger on today's cultural/denominational attitude toward the miraculous:

> Our Gospels reflect the delight which the first proclaimers of the Christ took in the miracle. The miracle was for the first church a part of the dramatic chiaroscuro which made clear the contours of the

Christ. In the miracles the beggary of man and the largesse of God were strikingly and unmistakably delineated, so that each miracle became the Gospel in miniature and was so proclaimed. The embarrassed fumbling with the miraculous which is characteristic of so much present-day theology is but one of a number of indications that the church's teaching and preaching has become sicklied o'er by the pale cast of thought and can deal only inadequately with the bright and plastic world of divine revelation. The miracles were once the church's delight and gave vigor to her faith. There is little ground for a feeling of modern complacency in a church whose teachers somehow give the impression that they would be happier if they had a non-miraculous Christ for their Lord.[3]

I believe this "embarrassed fumbling with the miraculous" is why theological papers and scholastic debates, rather than simple Bible study, marked this time of examining the Renewal.

Rather than rejoicing and praising God for the wonderful things that He was doing in people's lives, the legalistic, theological mind was moved to unbelief and cynical questioning—in the LCMS case, questioning toward the defense of one's salvation. It was assumed that the Renewal was all about getting, focusing on, and enjoying miracles and spiritual highs (they called it a theology of *glory*), rather than about Jesus. But when you do what Jesus says in John 5:39–40 and come not just to His Word but to the goal of that Word—to Him personally—then wonderful, personal, subjective, yes, but real experiences of the divine happen in your life. These are the *result* of faith, not the *goal*. The disciples on Pentecost were neither drunk with wine, nor tongues, nor other signs. Their fascination and excitement was with Jesus and the manifest presence of His Spirit. The tongues and other gifts were results not causes of their relationship with the Lord. And so they are today.

The objective Word is primary. He, through the Word, is the source and the goal of all things. But with that word come wonderful, subjective, miraculous revelations of the Christ. That's what Paul was saying in Galatians 3:1, 2, and 5:

> You foolish Galatians! Who has bewitched you? Before your very eyes Jesus Christ was clearly portrayed as crucified? I would like to learn just one thing from you: Did you receive the Spirit by observing the law, or by believing what you heard?....Does God give you his spirit and work miracles among you because you observe the law, or because you believe what you heard?

It is by hearing the Word of God and receiving by faith that the fullness of the Holy Spirit is received. It is by hearing the Word of God and walking in faith that the Spirit gives His gifts and works His miracles. And that fullness and those gifts are about sanctification—they are the result of the "believing what you heard" that Paul talks about in the scripture above, not the cause.

A few years ago I received a personal confirmation of this chapter's theme. I was talking on the telephone with Bob (not his real name), a member of the church I now serve as a part-time, retired associate pastor. Bob was a likable guy, a committed Christian, and an ultra-conservative activist for the old Missouri Synod and what I believe are its legalistic ways. Bob did much work in the church. He and his wife were some of the most regular and faithful attendees at Sunday services, adult Bible classes, and other meetings and gatherings. He helped me personally many times and I liked him. But when voter's meetings were held, a peculiar transformation would come upon Bob. He could be almost vicious. Of course, he was defending what he understood to be the truth. However, I learned from Bob as I talked to him on the phone, when it came to renewal, his unspoken but very real mantra was "Let's not study the Bible."

A couple of years ago we listed our congregation not only under the LCMS church listing but also under Charismatic churches. I had found in my previous parish that such a listing was an effective way to reach people in renewal who were looking to be part of a congregation that was both in a main-line denomination and open to the Spirit and His gifts. This listing became the most mentioned reason that visitors had chosen to join our congregation.

As soon as Bob discovered the charismatic listing he objected to the board of elders, indicating that *charismatic* was a term that identified the church with Pentecostalism and neo-Pentecostalism. Such an identification was not only misleading (we were not part of these denominations), he said, but unflattering. Bob, along with many LCMS members, seemed to have deeply-held prejudices against Pentecostals. I was there once. The elders responded from a report I made to them that said in part:

> I am unashamedly proud to be a Lutheran and char-
> ismatic, and I believe it is good for our church to have
> that same attitude and reputation. It combines what
> I believe is solid biblical theology (that's important—it

guards against deception) and zealous passion for the Lord's kingdom. Lutheran alone is thought by most to be stuffy and unfriendly (see Barna study which places Lutherans near the bottom in friendliness). Charismatic alone is not as negative a term, but can be, especially among main-line churches who may think of Charismatics as overly emotional and fanatical. The two together can be positively dynamite.

Charismatic is a great biblical word. It comes from the Greek word *charis*, which is translated "grace."[4] *Charisma* and *charismata* are translated as both "free gift," referring to God's free gift of forgiveness and salvation in Christ, and "gifts," as it appears five times in 1 Corinthians 12 to describe the spiritual gifts. Among those who have been involved in the charismatic movement it means various things:

- openness to the experiential power and gifts of the Holy Spirit

- a deepened devotion to and experience of Jesus as Savior and especially as Lord

- a hunger to read and study the Word of God

- a greater thirst for, freedom in, and joy from, communing with God in prayer and enthusiastic, expressive worship

- a greater appreciation for the fellowship of the saints

- a greater boldness in reaching out to the poor and the lost with the love and salvation of Christ Jesus

I have been involved in charismatic renewal for more than thirty-five years and have found the above to be true with very few exceptions. In listing our church as Charismatic as well as Lutheran in the directory, I hoped we would attract a lot of people interested in renewal and, in fact, sought to develop fully charismatic Lutherans through our Christian education and discipleship.

Bob rarely takes no for an answer when truth is at stake—a commendable practice, if you happen to know the truth. Bob was not impressed with our answer and began to send letters to our district president, the district board of directors, and to our synodical president. Our district president arranged for our circuit counselor along with a couple of other pastors to meet with Bob, me, and the chairman of our congregation. They listened to Bob's objections and to our reasons for the directory listing and responded the same way most everyone did (with the exception of the synodical president), namely, that the issue was a local congregational matter and not something that district or synod should get involved in.

Concerning church government, the LCMS has historically been congregational, not hierarchical. That is, in the LCMS the local congregation is autonomous (in charge of their own affairs and not to be interfered with by outside political entities), except in cases of heretical or immoral teaching or practice. Some in the Synod believe that parts of the Renewal are not doctrinally pure, but the Synod has not, as yet, declared that we in RIM have denied Christ and are preaching another gospel.

However, our new synodical president at the time

appeared to be against anything that went beyond the boundaries of traditional LCMS worship and practice, even though no part of the Renewal suggested a compromise of our Confessions or biblical truth. He was leading a crusade in the Synod to return to the old days and the old ways. In a synodical convention just before this event took place, the synodical president was given extraordinary leverage to interfere in local matters: a resolution made it possible for him to unseat district presidents if they are found by the denominational leadership to be remiss in their duties!

But what about Bob? you might ask. Shortly thereafter we learned that if Bob continued to write to our synodical president, the president would likely appoint an investigation team to look into the situation, and the district president would be brought in to make a judgment in the case.

I made an appointment with Bob, hoping that he and I could talk and pray about the situation and reach some agreement. At our meeting with the circuit counselor, Bob had passed out a fundamentalist periodical on Pentecostalism and neo-Pentecostalism. I read through it and discovered that its theological content was neither Lutheran nor biblical, and it was mostly filled with falsehood. Bob and I went through it point by point, but it didn't matter that it was filled with untruths. The reason, he said, for passing it out was to show that there was a connection between Pentecostalism and neo-Pentecostalism. After two hours together, I asked if we could meet again, but he declined because his mind was made up and I was not going to change my position. I shared with him my concern about putting our district president on the spot, but he insisted he would have to write his letters if the ads were not removed. I told him I would bring the issue back to the elders.

The elders and pastors had agreed all along that this issue was relatively insignificant and not worth the time and energy to defend. Further, we knew that the ad was effective and that giving in to manipulation may not be a godly choice. However, concern for our district president won out, and we agreed to cancel the offending yellow page listings.

Bob called me concerning the elders' decision and we talked for another hour and a half with the same result. I reiterated my concerns and pleaded with him to stop being a divisive element in the body and submit himself to the elders and pastors of the church. I asked him if he would be willing to study the Bible together. He refused! I told him that he was welcome to bring any of his pastor friends to our discussion, but he still declined my offer.

It brings me great sadness that our beloved LCMS has come to such a state. Oh, for a Berean heart and mind! (See Acts 17:11.)

Chapter 17

CHINESE WATER TORTURE

I WAS READING THROUGH the history of the passion of our Lord in chapters 26 and 27 of Matthew's Gospel when I was struck by the gradual but constant, relentless build up of rejection Jesus endured in His last hours. As a human being who was tempted in every way as we are, with feelings, longings, and needs like our own, Jesus endured a steamroller of emotional and physical pain. Note how the pressure builds from the Garden of Gethsemane to the cross. One after another, His disciples and followers forsook Him, leave Him, fail Him, betray Him, and mock Him. Of course, that was nothing compared to the spiritual agony of enduring the wrath of the Father as He carried the guilt of our sins, but our human minds help us better identify with the former struggles. I have titled these human physical and emotional agonies "Twelve Steps on the Way to Hell:"

1. Jesus told His disciples on the way to Gethsemane that they would "all fall away on account of [Him]" that night (Matt. 26:31). They strongly objected and, led by Peter, said they would never fall away from Him.

2. In Gethsemane Jesus asked Peter, James, and John to watch with Him for an hour, but they fell asleep (Matt. 26:36–45, rsv). Notice how many times Jesus repeats "with me" in this section. He was counting on His friends to watch with Him, be with Him—*help Him*—but they fell asleep again and again. They failed Him in His hour of need.

3. Then one of His chosen, Judas, betrayed Jesus with a kiss, though Jesus addressed Him as "friend" (Matt. 26:47–50).

4. When the authorities came to take Jesus away, "all the disciples deserted him and fled" (Matt. 26:56).

5. Next His religious authorities sought false witnesses against Him. (See Matthew 26:59.)

6. They accused him of blasphemy, and then they themselves blasphemed as they "spit in His face and struck Him with their fists…slapped him and said, 'Prophesy to us, Christ! Who hit you?'" (Matt. 26:67–68).

7. Peter then denied Him, just as Jesus had foretold. (See Matthew 26:69–75.)

8. Pontius Pilate, the civil authority appointed to see that justice prevailed, knew Jesus was innocent, but refused to release Him for fear of the crowd. Instead he asked them to choose between

Jesus and a hardened criminal, Barabbas. (See Matthew 27:11–24.)

9. The crowd chose to release Barabbas, shouting again and again for Pilate to "crucify Him!" (Matt. 27:22–23). He whom the crowds had followed, he who had blessed and healed them was suddenly the object of their scorn.

10. The cowardly Pilate had Jesus flogged, a cruel and painful ordeal reserved in Roman law for murderers and traitors. (See Matthew 27:26.)

11. Then the soldiers who were charged with keeping law and order pounced upon Him. Mocking His kingship, they dressed Jesus in a scarlet robe, thrust a crown of thorns upon His head, and gave Him a reed for a scepter. They taunted Him by kneeling down before Him in mock reverence, spitting on Him, and hitting Him. (See Matthew 27:27–31).

12. As Jesus was carrying His cross to Calvary, passersby on the busy road He traveled derided Him. Once He arrived, the religious leaders continued to mock Him, and even the robbers being crucified beside Him reviled Him. (See Matthew 27:32–44.)

As I read through these chapters and saw how this avalanche of hatred and rejection kept growing, weighing Him down, I asked myself what I would have done. If He were really tempted like we are tempted—and the Bible says

He was (Heb. 4:15)—then I assume that he felt great temptation not to turn the other cheek, to explode with hatred and vengeance, or to give up in discouragement and despair. But if He had done any of those things, we would be lost forever. That's why I believe that the story of the passion of Christ presents the spiritual battle of the ages. If Jesus would not have "humbled himself and [become] obedient to death" (Phil. 2:8), but would have instead turned from the will of His Father and gone His own way, acting as most all of us would have, we would have no hope. In that case, Jesus would have had to die for His own sin and couldn't have died for ours. But the suffering servant did not "falter or [become] discouraged" (Isa. 42:4).

His response to the injustice and agony He had suffered? Three sentences of concern for others. Even through the most intense abuse and rejection, there is no record of Him saying anything negative to His persecutors! Only when He was on the cross did He finally open his mouth: "Father, forgive them...." (Luke 23:34). That is such an unbelievable response that there is no need to question its genuineness. The same is true of His next words: "Today, you will be with me in paradise," spoken to one of the criminals at His side, and to Mary and John, "'Dear woman, here is your son...Here is your mother,'" (Luke 23:43 and John 19:26–27).

Then came the most hellish of rejections as He asked, "My God, my God, why have you forsaken me?" (Matt. 27:46). He was rejected by God the Father! The previous experiences of rejection were twelve steps *toward* hell. The suffering that led up to the cross was not the primary payment for our sin. As terrible as those twelve steps were, many have endured as much. But by choosing to carry the guilt of the world's sin upon His shoulders, Jesus was separated from and forsaken by the Father. I believe it was at this point in His passion that He made atonement for the sins of the world. He suffered and endured the pain of hell in our place. Everything else is insignificant compared to this. And He did it for us.

I share these twelve steps because I believe it is typical of the Enemy's tactics to get us away from the Father. Often, little by little, he tries to wear down the saints. I believe that is the tactic he used on us in Centerville. I am in no way suggesting that our troubles were remotely comparable to the agony of our Lord and to the myriads of martyrs of past and present history. I am simply saying that it can be helpful to know how the Enemy works. This chapter will chronicle the tactics he used to try to wear us down.

As the students returned in the fall and the prayer meetings began again, Pastor Schmidt's opposition to our gatherings and our involvement in charismatic renewal accelerated. I've already mentioned that Donnie and I agreed that we would stop going to Full Gospel Men's Fellowship International meetings and other such gatherings until we had opportunity to study the Scriptures applicable to the issues involved. However, the study of the Bible at elders meetings, once stopped, never got started again! Instead, elders meetings continued in the same pattern. Concerns were voiced about our prayer meetings, and those concerns became charges and, finally, restrictions that were passed down in the form of guidelines.

The guidelines were applied to small groups or home meetings. At first they suggested that all of what they termed the "special gifts," such as tongues, prophecy, and healing, should be halted until the issues surrounding their practice in the congregation were settled in order to avoid offending people. Even though it would be impossible to give offense (in the biblical sense of the word) by doing godly things, Donnie and I once again agreed to adhere to the guidelines because they came with the promise that the congregation would study the scriptural basis for the Renewal together. Finally, we were asked to stop the meetings in our home for the sake of unity and harmony in the church. We reluctantly agreed, optimistically believing that the congregation Bible studies on the topic would lead to our meetings being approved once again.

I am sure that what we were experiencing was not as bad as any ancient Chinese water torture, nor could it be compared in any way with what Jesus went through. However, the Enemy's tactic was the same. Slowly and inexorably, freedoms and blessings were withdrawn like the steady dropping of water from a carefully controlled faucet: worshiping at full gospel meetings was prohibited, as was the use of prayer language, any other spiritual gifts, and praying for healing. And no more prayer meetings in our home. We were in the wilderness again.

Nonetheless, there were no restrictions on the students. They immediately searched for another place to meet. St. Mark's Church predictably turned them down, but the local Episcopal church didn't. They began to meet there, of course, without us. A high school girl heard about the meetings on a night in which she was planning to kill herself and decided to look into what was going on. She was embraced by the young people, prayed for, born from above, and filled with the Holy Spirit. She became a committed member of this growing charismatic community. She probably would never have heard of the prayer meetings if they hadn't been at her church. God is so good. He continually takes whatever the Devil and the world can throw at Him and builds the kingdom in spite of it. How silly to fuss, fret, and feel sorry for one's self when God is in control and faithful to fulfill His promises.

During this time, I returned from a youth outing and walked into a boardroom to discover Pastor Schmidt and the elders seated around a table in deep discussion. As my mouth dropped open at having stumbled upon their secret meeting, their eyes stretched wide in surprise at seeing me. I quickly excused myself and left. I had just made a new pot of coffee, so I put it and some cups on a tray with cream and sugar and brought it all back into the boardroom to serve them. I then left and went about my usual Saturday business.

The whole experience served as yet another testimony to the faithfulness of God in my life. I once had a great fear of rejection. Much of the energy I put into former parishes was invested as much for acceptance and to build my reputation as a successful minister as it was out of pure devotion to God and His purposes. I'm not saying I didn't have to fight fear at times in Centerville, but on the whole, God had worked in me a trust in Him that overcame the fear I once held and enabled me to truly love those who seemed to be set on hurting me.

The fact that I had once believed as Pastor Schmidt and the elders did helped me to better understand that their motives were pure, even if their tactics were sometimes ungodly. I remember calling on one of the church members, the wife of a college department head, who began to criticize Pastor Schmidt. I found myself coming to his defense, pointing out that he really believed that what he and the elders were doing was right.

Chapter 18

THE DEVIL'S TONGUES MOVEMENT

ONE EVENING I got a call from a brother pastor in Colorado. His opening remarks were, "I heard something about you the other day and I want to check it out with you to see if it is true. Someone told me that a couple weeks ago you prayed with a man for healing and counseled him to throw away his medicine. He then went out on the highway, had a seizure, wrecked his car, and was killed."

I knew right away what he was talking about. It was one of the many stories that circulated in and beyond our town when it became known that I was "one of those fanatical Charismatics" who prayed for the sick and expected God to heal them. But as usual, not all the facts were straight. First of all it wasn't I who prayed for the individual. I wasn't even in the same town at the time. Further, he was not counseled to throw away his medicine. In fact, when he called me up and asked if he should stop taking his medicine, I advised him to confirm with his physician whatever healing had taken place and follow his orders. During a visit to the doctor shortly thereafter, the physician did reduce the medication, but the man continued taking that medicine. Though he did die while driving his car, his death was caused by a heart attack, not an accident. Finally, the incident didn't happen a couple of weeks ago, as my pastor friend indicated. It happened almost three years before he called me.

During this time one of the most common charges leveled against the Charismatic movement was that it divided churches. It was my experience that it did just the opposite. It unites. But there is a tongues movement that does divide. It is the devil's tongues movement—gossip. Through this divisive tongues movement, the devil not only seeks to make the gospel ineffective by showing to a laughing world a divided and backbiting church, but he also seeks to attack the gospel itself. Paul, in his letter to the Ephesians, especially Ephesians 2:11 and 3:6, points out that part of the mystery of the gospel is that God's grace in Christ is for everyone. Jesus not only has made us one with Him, but he has made us one with one another. The cross has not only knocked down the barriers between us and God, it has knocked down the barriers that divide people from one another.

The devil has two whispering campaigns. As the great accuser of the brethren, he is always seeking to whisper into our ears and tell us how sinful and unlovable we are. With that he seeks to build up walls of guilt between God and us. The cross takes care of that by proving God's love for us and washing away our guilt. We can send the devil back to hell, but we need to fight his other whispering campaign too, the one in which he seeks to get us to talk about our brothers and sisters and thus build back the walls that Jesus removed when He joined us all together in one body.

Through both attacks, Satan seeks to destroy the Word and work of Christ. Gossip is, therefore, no small thing. Gossip is nothing less than the devil's attack upon the gospel itself. James was not exaggerating, then, when he said that the tongue is "a restless evil, full of deadly poison" (James 3:8).

I have noticed that the Charismatic movement does unite. In my strict Missouri Synod Lutheran background, I participated in and taught many confirmation classes, both youth and adult. These classes were helpful in providing a foundation of teaching on the basic truths of Christianity. However, there were aspects of these classes that were simply training in bigotry. They built walls. For instance, when pointing out our understanding of the sacraments it was automatic to point out the errors of other denominations: "The Baptists down the block don't believe in infant baptism." We did not emphasize the oneness of the body of Christ or the fact that even if they didn't believe in infant baptism we were still one in Christ. They were (and are) our brothers and sisters in the family of God.

When the grace of God brought me into the fullness of the Holy Spirit, I began to see (by getting acquainted with them) that members of other denominations were really Christians. Many of them, especially those I met at charismatic meetings, loved the Lord Jesus and desired to live for Him and serve Him with all their hearts. They worshiped Him in Spirit and in truth. In fact, I saw that many Lutherans who knew and believed all the "right doctrines" seemed almost dead compared to these newfound brothers and sisters with all their "errors." God, through the Charismatic Renewal, caused me to see the unity of the church. I had been denying Christ in my brothers, and it was the Lord's tongues movement which was instrumental in bringing the barriers down in my heart. The Charismatic movement does unite. It unites because it is a movement of the Holy Spirit and the chief work of the Spirit is to exalt Jesus as Savior and Lord. I have never met anyone who has been touched by the Holy Spirit who was not in love with Jesus. I remember a call I made to a Roman Catholic seminary in Steubenville, Ohio. It was a Roman Catholic center of renewal in the Holy Spirit and had published a book on the Spirit that I wanted to order. On the phone I told them I was a Lutheran Pastor and immediately they excitedly responded, "Luther was right! Jesus is the only way. It is not by our works or efforts. Salvation is by grace alone through faith in Jesus and His sacrifice on the cross for us."

Yet there sometimes does seem to be division within some churches when members become involved in the Renewal. It has been my experience that there are different reasons for this. Usually there is already some division in the congregation. Renewal simply brings it to the surface. Also, when either those who have had charismatic experiences or those who haven't had them become militant and exclusive, division occurs. No matter what the contributing factors, however, gossip is the one common ingredient that cements the wall of separation between brothers and brings shame and scandal to the body of Christ.

Following are a few principles or attitudes which I feel

need to be adopted and followed by all Christians who want the walls of separation to remain down so that Jesus may be glorified.

The first step must be to set our minds on things that are above. The central work of Satan is to direct our attention and our trust away from Jesus. The devil wants us to be absorbed in ourselves, particularly our needs and desires. Concerning others, he wants to emphasize our differences and cause us to focus on the real or imagined faults of others. Our relationships with people spring from our relationship with God. The truth of the gospel is that the barriers are down between God and us. We were "buried with him in baptism and raised with him.... God made you alive with Christ. He forgive us all our sins (Col. 2:12–13). That is where it starts. Holding firm to that truth, we can follow Paul's advice: "If then you have been raised with Christ, seek the things that are above, where Christ is" (Col. 3:1–2, RSV). When you set your mind on Christ, your lips will follow and you will put away all "anger, rage, malice, slander, and filthy talk from your mouths" (Col. 3:8).

Catch a vision of the unity of the church. There is only one church. (See Ephesians 4:4–6.) The implications of that truth are sometimes lost. The fact that the church is one means that we don't have to strive for unity. We already have it; it simply needs to be maintained. (Ephesians 4:3.) That the church is one means we are to look upon all those who believe in Jesus as Savior as one with us and members of the same body in the Lord. It also means that in spite of doctrinal differences, racial differences, and national and cultural differences, we are brothers and sisters in Christ and we should act like it. This does not mean the differences are unimportant, nor does it mean that we should water down our own convictions. But it does mean that we should love our brothers from our hearts and accept them as children of the Father with whom we will spend eternity.

When a brother or sister is denying Christ through manifest sin or teaching which is contrary to the gospel, there are some practical things Jesus calls us to in Matthew 18:15–17. The three steps Jesus records there not only serve as an effective guard against the devil's divisive efforts, but will bring healing and life.

According to this scripture, the first course of action if your brother sins against you is to go and tell him his fault between you and him alone. If it is an unbeliever who has sinned against you, it is godly to turn the other cheek and return good for the evil done to you. However, when a fellow believer sins, another avenue is to be taken. Your brother needs help, and if you avoid dealing with his sin he will not be helped. You are to go in love to him in order that he might receive the grace of God that will rescue him from his sin. Jesus says to talk to him alone, not to the elders, the pastor, his relatives, or neighbors. To talk to anyone else is gossip. As you go and talk to him alone, you may find that what you thought was terrible, wasn't. You simply misunderstood. Even if you did not misunderstand and his action was truly negative, you may find he is relieved to have you come and speak to him and offer your help and concern.

If your brother isn't relieved but is instead hurt, offended, or defensive, he is to be pitied, not feared. Jesus provides another step for such a response. We are to take one or two others with us to talk to him. Remember that you go as the chief of sinners. Every Christian can say with St. Paul, "I'm the worst sinner I know" (1 Tim. 1:15, author's paraphrase), because each of us knows our own sins far better than we know anyone else's. What business does the world's worst sinner have in attempting to meddle in someone else's life? An evangelism maxim fits: "We are all beggars telling other beggars where to find bread." That Bread of Life is Jesus. Whether they know it or not, everybody is desperately in need of Jesus. A believer who doesn't want to repent of his sins needs the touch of the Lord Jesus as Savior and as the final judge of sin.

If he still doesn't listen and repent of a manifest sin or an open denial of Christ, then you take it to the congregation. "If he refuses to listen even to the church, treat him as you would a pagan or a tax collector" (Matt. 18:17). That is, put him on the prospect list. You pray and work for his conversion to Christ, but you still don't talk about him, except to God.

Gossip is sometimes called "the Christian sin." Oh, if only that were a complete lie! But unfortunately we all continue to fail to be the perfect light God would have us be. My prayer is that my story will bring true repentance and Spirit-empowered change to our hearts and lives, especially in this area of talking ill about others, fallen or saved.

Chapter 19

THAT DREADFUL
VOTER'S MEETING

WE READ IN the Bible that God did a lot of speaking to His people through dreams. I rarely ever remember dreams, but shortly after Pastor Schmidt came to Centerville I had three dreams that I remembered vividly. I believe God was talking to me through them to comfort and encourage Donnie and me and our little charismatic community. The dreams occurred toward the end of the approximately nine months of elders meetings described in the last chapter. The congregation had not yet become involved in those issues, except through rumor and gossip. I share the dreams as another example of the faithfulness of God, who continues His work in spite of the failures of man.

In the first dream I was shopping in downtown Centerville at the local variety store. I parked my car, and although at the time I owned a Volkswagen bus the car in my dream was a Volkswagen bug. I parked it at the side entrance of the store. When I came out, it was gone. I was disturbed. I went around the corner and there I found it, buried up to the windows in a bank of snow. The snow had even gotten inside the car. The thought that came to me in the dream was: "Do not let them take away what you have."

Shortly after that dream, a brother in Minneapolis called and said that the Lord had brought to his attention the account of the Philadelphia church in Revelation 3:7 so that it could be a comfort to us. A few days later, a brother from Colorado called to tell us that the Lord gave him the same verse to share with us. We were excited and in awe. Then at our prayer meeting that week, a traveler passing through town came to the meeting (we often had strangers drop in) and told us before the evening was over that the Lord had given him the passage from Revelation 3:7 to give to us as possibly applicable to something we were going through. God was trying to tell us something.

> And to the angel of the church at Philadelphia write: "The words of the holy one, the true one, who has the key of David, who opens and no one shall shut, who shuts and no one opens. I know your works. Behold, I have set before you an open door, which no one is able to shut; I know that you have but little power, and yet you have kept my word and have not denied my name. Behold, I will make those of the synagogue of Satan who say that they that are Jews and are not, but lie—behold, I will make them come and bow down before your feet, and learn that I have loved you. Because you have kept my word of patient endurance, I will keep you from the hour of trial which is coming on the whole world, to try those who dwell upon the earth. I am coming soon; hold fast what you have, so that no one may seize your crown. He who conquers, I will make him a pillar in the temple of my God; never

shall he go out of it, and I will write on him the name of my God, and the name of the city of my God, the new Jerusalem which comes down from my God out of heaven, and my own new name. He who has an ear, let him hear what the Spirit says to the churches."

—Revelation 3:7–13, RSV

The biblical rule for testimony is that an issue must be confirmed by two or three witnesses. (See Matthew 18:16 and Deuteronomy 19:15.) Three were given to us. God is faithful! We and the students were excited that the Lord should so clearly speak to us and, in effect, confirm that He really was behind what we believed He was doing in us. Although parts of the Philadelphia letter were not applicable to our lives, much of it fit right in with my dreams. He did set before us an "open door which no one shall shut." In fact, in spite of the pressure of some of the powers that were operating at the time, the prayer meetings we started many years ago are today still bringing praise and glory to God and spiritual growth and healing to those involved.

The letter also said that the group of believers in Philadelphia had "little power." A Volkswagen bug—the car in my dream—has little power. The emphasis in our prayer meetings was on guidance, the glory and free expression of worship in and through the Holy Spirit, and cultivating deeper relationships with God and one another. There were not many powerful, miraculous signs in our fellowship.

It is clear in the letter to the church at Philadelphia that there was an opposition group that was seeking to take away what they had. (See Revelation 3:9.) Similarly, in the dream my Volkswagen bug was moved from the side to the front of the store and then covered and filled with snow. Snow is the antithesis of the Holy Spirit's fire. The words in the dream were "do not let them take away what you have." The angel of the Lord cautioned the Philadelphia church to "hold fast to what you have, so that no one may seize your crown" (Rev. 3:11).

Weeks after this dream and the confirmations that followed it, I had another dream in which a pesky little dog kept nipping at me and taking little bites at my feet. Although the dog was cute, it soon began to annoy me. After repeated scoldings and comic attempts to dodge it, I finally had to pick him up and give him a spanking. As I woke up, I thought of John Schmidt! I know that is a terrible presumption to personify my co-pastor as a cute but nasty little dog, but the fact of the matter is that he had been bringing accusations and charges against me into elders meetings for six months; charges that I am convinced were a twisting of the truth and at best an un-brotherly attack upon my person and ministry, finally resulting in that dreadful voters meeting. I took from this dream that it would, perhaps, be necessary to confront Pastor Schmidt with the things he was doing. I typed up a list of concerns related to his actions toward and concerning me and gave him a copy.

In that list I mentioned how Jesus' teaching on church discipline in Matthew 18:15–20 was not followed. Instead of speaking to the Board of Elders, anyone who has something against a brother or sister should address it privately with that person. If he or she doesn't listen or still disagrees, then two or three other witnesses may be brought along to initiate another discussion. This did not happen. Further, most if not all of the charges brought against me were either untrue or a twisting of the truth. I also explained that he was speaking against godly activities—our prayer meetings, Spirit-led worship, testimonies of God's grace, Bible study, and the use of the gifts of the Spirit—that, though culturally strange, are solidly biblical. Although I was sure he felt strongly that he was acting according to God's will, I encouraged him to consider the possibility that God was behind this renewal. (See Acts 5:39.)

At the time, I did not understand those first two dreams at all. They were, like the Bible's apocalyptic literature, in symbol such that I wasn't sure what they meant. Nonetheless, they remained salient in my memory in a way that no other dreams have.

It was shortly after these dreams that Pastor Schmidt arranged for a meeting on August 31—my and Donnie's wedding anniversary—with the elders and the LCMS district president, who, as I mentioned earlier, was also a member of our congregation. The purpose of the meeting was to bring formal charges against me in order to ask for my resignation as pastor of St. Mark's. (See Appendix II for a full copy of the charges.)

An elder approached me the night before the meeting and handed me a rather lengthy document. The top of the first page said, "Presented by the elders to Pastor Dorpat on August 31." As I looked at the date, I realized that the elder had given me the list of charges a day early. Can you imagine receiving a long list of charges that are meant to prove that you are not only bordering on heretical, but also sly, rebellious, and inept in your calling? This dear brother was helping me to be prepared intellectually as well as emotionally for the meeting scheduled for the next evening. I am grateful for that elder and his sense of fairness in extending me the opportunity to react to such accusations in private before having to offer a response in defense.

The introduction to my written response to the charges follows. (See Appendix III for my complete response.)

> First of all, I appreciate the time you are all taking to come here. I believe you have the best interests of the kingdom of God at heart although I also believe you are misled. But I do believe your intentions are honorable and I praise God for that.
>
> I also thank you for the chance to look at the charges that you have lined up. These were given to me last night after the Voter's Meeting. That is poor politics but it is what a loving Christian brother would do. The political manipulator, of course, would have tried to get all the shock value out of the charges that he could. He would seek to ignore the dictates of our Lord in Matthew 18 to go to the brother alone with concerns and lovingly admonish him in order to win him. He would rather seek to drop the accusations like a bomb with others present, so that the opponent would feel threatened and would be led to react in an emotional, frightened state and would say things that he would not ordinarily say. Then, of course, those statements, too, could be used against him. But you have refused to act politically. Like Christian brothers you have given these to me ahead of time that I might have a little time to look at them and prepare a response. Thank you.

I believe those charges are more a shock to me today than they were when I first received them. Some of the events I remember well. I have no recollection of other episodes mentioned in the charges. I still feel that the intent of my co-pastor and perhaps one of the elders (though clearly not the one who offered me the advance copy of the charges) was to drop these charges on me like a bomb with the district president in attendance. It seemed to me that my co-pastor and the elder were not being very faithful. In fact my impression was that they were rather being judgmental, deceitful, and downright mean. However, as you can tell from the sarcasm above, I was not without fault.

The three major categories of the charges were:

I. Unionism contrary to the constitution and practices of the congregation and synod

II. Doctrinal concerns

III. Offensive Conduct

The description of offenses under the charge of unionism included two examples: an announcement I made during a sermon that I had prayed with a Catholic priest and my participation in an interdenominational meeting in a nearby town. I am fully convinced that most all of the charges were specifically from Pastor Schmidt. However, this one in particular may have been suggested by members of the congregation.

This was my response to the charge that I prayed with a Catholic priest:

In that same sermon it was pointed out that this was at [our own Lutheran] Concordia Seminary, that it was not in a worship service and that it was in a Lutheran setting, that this priest simply wanted to thank God with someone because he had finally come to know Jesus Christ as savior and Lord. To call that unionism, offensive, and a sin, is nothing short of twisting the intentions of God's Word. And the very idea of putting this down here as a charge, would indicate to me (and I believe, to any other fair-minded, evangelical Christian), a spirit of deceit and sinful judging. Rather than listing this as a charge it would seem to me to be the duty of the pastors and elders of St Mark to point out the beauty of such an occurrence and to correct the false interpretations of such a self-righteous, judging attitude. If angels in heaven rejoice over one sinner who repents shouldn't we? The person who would judge that to be a sin, is himself, as Jesus would say, in danger of being judged.

My response to this charge shows that my attitude was often not the best. I wasn't rejoicing much in my suffering (see Matthew 5:11–12 and Luke 6:22). I believe I spoke the truth in that response, but it wasn't speaking the truth in love. Pastor Schmidt, the elders, and I exacerbated our conflict by failing at times to act in love and follow biblical guidelines on how to deal with conflicts. (See Matthew 5:23–24 and 18:15.) Perhaps the above charge and many others could have been laid to rest if we had obeyed the Word's instructions regarding these situations. Thankfully, those same verses that provide instructions also illustrate how God is faithful, even when his people aren't.

The other unionism charge was about my involvement in a local interdenominational meeting. Our denomination recognizes that there can be disagreement among LCMS members and theologians on doctrines that do not directly impact on one's salvation. However, both lay members and clergy are expected to live their lives in obedience to the doctrines of the church, even those that we might not agree with. For a long time I had disagreed with our denomination's position on unionism, but for the sake of harmony and loyalty, I was careful to not act contrary to our church's teaching. This interdenominational meeting might have seemed to be an exception. It would not be considered unionism to merely attend such a meeting. However, when I got there I was publicly asked to open the meeting with prayer. Back then taking part in the leadership of a worship service that included other leaders with whom we are not in complete doctrinal agreement would likely have been considered unionism. But I felt it would have been a worse witness to Christ and my relationship with Him to refuse their impromptu offer than it would have been to accept it, so I began the meeting with a biblical prayer.

After going through the charges and my corresponding responses, the LCMS district president remarked that, as far as he was concerned, I had satisfactorily addressed all the areas of concern! Now Pastor Schmidt and the elders were in quite a quandary. The whole congregation and, I suspect, much of the town, was in an uproar. The voters meeting was scheduled, but they no longer had charges to bring against me!

Having agreed that they could no longer uphold the

request for my resignation after the district president dropped all charges against me, the Board of Elders decided that instead I should resign, because the talk surrounding the controversy would prevent me from ministering effectively in the congregation. However, I respectfully refused to resign. I felt the congregation needed to face the issues of the Renewal movement through a biblical study of the charismata and should not try to dodge those realities by simply getting rid of me.

The night of the voters meeting arrived. Though just under two hundred voters were present, hundreds of non-voting observers nearly filled the one thousand-seat sanctuary. (To vote at this meeting, a person had to be male, over the age of twenty-one, a member of the congregation, and had to have joined the voter's assembly at a previous meeting.) The Board of Elders presented their resolution to ask for my resignation. An expert from the college pointed out that the vote on such an issue would require a two-thirds majority to pass. When I was given the floor, I continued to speak against the resolution because I believed, as I said above, that we should get into the Word and deal with the issues of the movement. It wasn't going to go away, and I was hopeful that the congregation could work together as brothers and sisters in Christ to come to some kind of peaceful, godly resolution. (See Appendix IV for the complete text of my remarks to the voters at this meeting.)

Many of the voters and other attendees peppered the evening with questions. "Why was this happening?" "What has Pastor Dorpat done?" "Were there any specific charges against him?" The elders explained that charges had been brought, but that I had answered them satisfactorily and therefore it would not be right to repeat them. At this point, Pastor Schmidt could stand it no longer. He got up to a microphone and quickly read off the charges anyway!

The vote was taken: 107 in favor of my dismissal and 64 opposed, just 7 short of a two-thirds majority. I was allowed to stay!

Following this announcement, Pastor Schmidt got up and said that because "the congregation voted for the Charismatic movement" he could not stay in the congregation. He then immediately declared his resignation and briskly marched out of the sanctuary. The meeting was then quickly concluded.

The last of the three dreams I had during that season applies directly to that voters meeting. I saw a man facing me, saying he had "lost the gamble." With his arms and hands reaching toward me, palms up (as if he was giving me something), he pointed over his shoulder to a house. "Here; it's yours," he said of the estate. "Take it. I lost. I lost the gamble." I, in return, refused to accept it, saying, "No, no, I can't accept it. I can't take it. I can't take it. No, no." I know that it might seem a stretch to suggest that a mansion could be likened to the function of shepherding a congregation. However, the man's insistence signaled that he was giving up. He was quitting, just as my co-pastor had done.

Pastor Schmidt's public resignation left me as the only pastor of St. Mark's. I could have seen this as a golden opportunity, but I didn't. I was shaken by it all. Though I was not forced to resign, there remained a number of people that wanted me out. I walked down the center aisle after that voters meeting and was confronted by scowls and hateful looks from people whom I loved, whom I had prayed with and ministered to. One man that I counted as a dear friend came up to me in a rage asking me how I could do such a thing, how I could bring such division in the church by my rebellion. "Why didn't you obey Pastor Schmidt? He was in charge," he said. When I arrived home, I half expected a brick to come through the window! And yet, in spite of the anger expressed toward me and the resulting deep disappointment I felt, the whole evening was full of a completely unexpected but very real peace that I can attribute only to God.

Why didn't I obey Pastor Schmidt? I wish I had contacted the brother who asked me that question on that awful evening so that I could explain to him that Donnie and I had obeyed Pastor Schmidt and the Board of Elders. They had passed resolutions that, step by step, called for us to give up godly, biblical activities. Donnie and I prayed and decided to obey those requests, though it was very painful for us. In spite of the pressure, we continued to enjoy the Lord and ultimately realized the truth that "in all things God works for the good of those who love him" (Rom. 8:28). Though difficult, they were times of growth, as they drove us to our knees and to a more complete dependence on our God.

The atmosphere at our home after that dreadful voters meeting was sober, yet relaxed (although I purposely didn't sit too close to the window). A few of the students came over to comfort and encourage us. We prayed together briefly for the congregation, the elders, and the Schmidt family, being careful that our actions did not break our promise to discontinue participating in the prayer meetings once held at our house.

It wasn't long before I felt the Lord was telling me to resign as pastor of St. Mark's Lutheran Church. A number of people had lovingly approached me to confirm the wisdom of that decision, so I formulated a letter to the Board of Elders tendering my resignation. My main concern was the fact that well over a majority of the congregation had voted that I should leave. The elders had said earlier that I wouldn't be able to minister effectively because of the talk about the Renewal. Perhaps they were right. At any rate, I was weary with the battle and figured the days ahead would be even more difficult. I hoped that my leaving would open the door for a pastor that would bring real healing to this precious body of believers.

An immediate benefit of my resignation was the re-establishment of the weekly prayer meetings in our home. What joy there was in our home as the students were once again together worshiping and praising God with us, sharing His word, and corporately praying for one another!

Chapter 20

SEVEN KIDS AND OUT OF WORK

LTHOUGH THE ORDEAL was quite a blow to my ego, it was also a blessed opportunity to grow up into Christ. How infinitely more painful was Jesus' suffering at the hands of His people, and He did it for me. My troubles fade into insignificance when I think of the price He paid on the cross so that I could know Him intimately.

St. Mark's accepted my resignation. Knowing it would be a long time before another congregation would extend me a call—that is, if another congregation would even consider me for such a position—they offered to pay my regular salary for over three and a half months or until I found other employment. Just in case I didn't receive another call right away, I immediately put a resume together and started looking for a job. But even secular jobs were not readily available. When I submitted my resume to an organization in a larger, neighboring city, I saw them add mine to the bottom of a large stack of resumes that had already been submitted to them.

In the meantime, many of our friends stepped in to help and act as an extension of God's hand over our family. Some of our church family brought food over for us—sometimes bags of groceries, sometimes a prepared dinner. More than once, I discovered an envelope filled with cash in our mailbox. One day a local doctor (not a member of our church) plowed the snow off our driveway, free of charge. The professors and their families were especially helpful, inviting us over for dinner and befriending us in many ways. The president of the college, almost apologetically, gave me the rather monotonous job of putting all the student records on microfiche, but I happily accepted, thus keeping the wolves at bay.

Finally in March of that year, a church member, who worked closely for the state governor, got me the job of senior health planner in the state capital office of Comprehensive Health Planning, part of the State Health Department.

God provided through His people, but He also seemed to miraculously provide for us directly. That first year at the health department was the only year in our marriage that our family of nine was not covered with health insurance. As I was filling out my income tax form at the beginning of the following year, I noticed the past year had been the first year in which we had no medical bills for that year—and no sickness either. We didn't even buy a bottle of aspirin that year, not because we couldn't afford it, but because we didn't need it.

It had been a few months since my resignation, and Donnie was beginning to gently warn me that perhaps the pastoral ministry part of my life was over. The common practice in our denomination is to ask another available pastor to fill in a vacancy when the local pastor is sick, goes on vacation, or while that church searches for a full-time pastor. I hadn't received any invitations to preach at other local parishes. She encouraged me to cash in our pension so that we would have money to buy food and other essentials. I insisted that I believed God wanted me to continue in the ministry, even though I was probably black-listed. I felt that congregations and pastors wouldn't want me to preach because of the notoriety of my leaving this influential church.

We were at a stalemate. Donnie quickly began to call out to God about our conflict. She later informed me that she told the Lord that she was concerned about the kids. "Lord, you know how I am," she said. "I'll just continue to badger Dave about this unless you make it clear to me what you want." The thought that the children might go hungry devastated her. Then an almost impossible scenario occurred to her: "Lord" she said, "If you want Dave to stay in the ministry, please get him a few invitations to preach at neighboring churches. Amen."

Within a week I had seven invitations to preach at various LCMS churches! This not only seemed to be a miraculous answer to her prayer, but it saved my pastoral reputation and pension. When a pastor resigns and accepts a secular job without continuing to participate in pastoral ministry, he is soon taken off the synodical pastoral list. And once off that list, it is very difficult to get back on. As long as I could show that I was still pastoring while waiting for a call from another church, I could go as long as three years before getting defrocked.

We were to remain in Centerville for another five and a half years. God had spoken to my heart that I was to stay as an active, supportive layman in the town and in St. Mark's congregation. Nonetheless, if a call would come from another congregation—however improbable it seemed—we would consider it. During that time, all the elders except one came to us and asked our forgiveness, some with tears. I continued to receive invitations to speak at summer camps, retreats, conferences, and to preach at various congregations around the area and beyond, thus enabling me to remain on the synodical pastoral list. But three years can go by pretty fast. As they did, my kind and very supporting district president submitted, each year, a recommendation that I be retained on the clergy roster. Was I finished as a pastor?

Chapter 21

IT'S GREAT TO BE
A LAYMAN!

ALTHOUGH OUR DISTRICT president put out the word that I was available for and needed a call to serve in a congregation, no calls came for a long time. While still looking for employment, I remembered that I had worked as a teamster in a bottling plant about fifteen years earlier in Spokane, Washington. I went to the teamster's office in a neighboring large town and showed the lady my withdrawal card. She said that business was very slow and I probably couldn't get anything more than a one-day job. I gave her my name and number, and the following Friday she called me up and said that there was a job for me at Ideal Trucking. I didn't have any real work clothes, so I wore an old pair of slacks and a jacket and bought some leather gloves.

"Here's the guy from the union!" That was my formal introduction to my fellow workers as I arrived at my new job. I noticed that they were looking me over as if to ask if I really belonged there. If I did, I certainly didn't feel like it. One of them asked, "Are you ready to go to work?" I answered that I was, so he directed me to take a pile of goods and load it on to a particular truck. I helped load trucks for three or more hours until the drivers all pulled away, ready to distribute their cargo around the city. I was left alone on the dock with only one other worker. He pointed toward the remaining vehicle and said to me, "That's your truck." When I arrived at work that day, I wondered if I would be required to drive a truck. I wondered if they knew how limited my experience was in that area. But it didn't seem to matter. The only trouble was that I had loaded everyone else's truck except my own. My co-worker gave me a clipboard with all the "bills of lading" and began to walk away. I felt very foolish having to ask what I was supposed to do, but I started with a barrage of questions: "Bills of lading?" "Which copy do I keep?" "Where is the address to deliver the freight?" "Where is the freight?" He kindly and patiently filled me in. I found my cargo at various places on the dock and in the building. I couldn't find some of them and had to report to the office for assistance. Finally, though, I got nearly everything loaded. I was all ready to go, except I didn't know how to lift the power tailgate. With my co-worker's help, I finally got on the road with my freight. I made all the deliveries without catastrophe.

It's wonderful to be able to live the Christian life and do ordinary things for Jesus Christ. To deliver goods for Him. To help load trucks for Him. All around me there was cursing, anger, unhappy people who didn't seem to know the Lord. I was so happy to be able to serve and witness to these men with my actions and life. I delivered my goods very quickly that first day and got back before any of the other trucks! I was able to work on the dock again—work some more for Jesus. What a glorious day it was. In spite of my clumsy attempt at trucking and the fact that I had been cursed at, apparently been taken advantage of, and somewhat humiliated that morning, on the way home I prayed that somehow I would be able to get a steady job that would allow me to work with people and, by the grace of God, lead them to a personal relationship with Jesus. I felt exhilarated by the freedom to be loving and friendly with no church rolls to build, no reputation to uphold, and no church council to be concerned about pleasing. I had discovered the joys of ministry as a layman.

It is, of course, also great to be a clergyman. As a clergyman there are great opportunities to minister to people in need. (Perhaps that is why many clergy are called "ministers.") However, there are situations where a pastor finds it harder to function in that ministry role than a layman would, and there are people who are much harder for him to reach. Preachers are often expected to witness and build their churches, so people often assume that a pastor has ulterior motives whenever he speaks about the gospel outside of the pulpit. A layman, on the other hand, knows that he might risk being called a fanatic or weird if he is open about his faith. For this reason, whatever ministry he does may be interpreted as more authentic or sincere than a pastor's.

Not long after my attempt at being a tough trucker, another opportunity arrived. I was hired to take inventory in a large department store not far from Centerville. My partner that day was a young and pretty sophomore from the state university. We worked together rather rapidly for over four hours, not exchanging much talk and keeping to the business at hand. It was rather cold out, so after we were through work I asked the young lady whether she would like to have a ride home. She accepted.

While leaving the store, she asked me what I did for a living. I told her that I had recently resigned from the pastorate of a parish in Centerville, and she discovered that we were of the same denomination. She was interested in the fact that one of the reasons for my resignation was my involvement in ministering to some "Jesus people" who were attending the college. As we were walking to the car we met her boyfriend. Upon hearing about my situation, he immediately told me that he was having real trouble relating to his church. They invited me to her apartment to talk. There we sat on the floor and talked about the Lord for over an hour. As a pastor I was expected to sound religious. But here I had come to know someone by working next to her, rubbing elbows with her, and now, as her equal, without any special interests or ulterior motives, I was able to share my Lord with her and her friend. And they received my witness.

I had often preached that the best person to win a farmer to Christ was another farmer; the best one to win a housewife for Christ was another housewife; a business man, another business man, etc. I could now add that the best one to win a part-time inventory-taker was another part-time inventory taker. As a pastor in a pulpit I would not have had that opportunity.

It is true that as a person works day after day at some job that doesn't seem to count for much, the monotony of it all can begin to weigh heavily. That person may begin to complain about the uselessness of the job and the pointlessness of life in general. But if that person would look around, he or she would find people who are carrying great burdens of worry, fear, and loneliness, to name a few struggles. Everybody needs Jesus. Opportunities abound for us to serve, love, or even simply speak kindly to people.

Chapter 22

IT'S GREAT TO BE
A CLERGYMAN!

I STARTED THIS BOOK many years ago and am now finally finishing it. If you have gotten this far in your reading, I hope and pray that what I have shared has brought you closer to Him. He loves you with an everlasting love. There isn't anything in your past or your present that He cannot help you with and deliver you from. He desires only your good. As the Scripture says, "God is love" (1 John 4:8, 16). Put another way, just as it is impossible for God not to love, it is likewise impossible for us to do anything to keep Him from loving us.

I wrote this book to communicate just that. God's love is the one great reality. It is so simple and yet, so wonderfully profound. God, from eternity, beyond all space and time, became one of us in order to win and woo a wayward, unfaithful people back to Him. In a mystery beyond our understanding, He, through His Son Jesus, endured an eternal hell upon the cross in our place. He suffered and died for us. He rose from the dead in order that His Spirit might come to dwell within us to help us grow up into His likeness, able to bring his life to a dying world through His Word and presence. Through Him we can experience free, unfettered worship, praise, thanksgiving, and adoration of the Prince. Love can overflow from our hearts to Him and to those in need of His life and forgiveness.

I am thankful for my Lutheran heritage. The reformation truth that all this life that has been given to us unworthy creatures has come to us only through God's grace and mercy. We don't deserve it at all. We deserve hell. But instead, because Jesus went there in our place to pay for our sins, as we put our trust in Him, we have eternal life and the tender, yet powerful peace and joy of the ever-present God, the Holy Spirit.

His other gifts are also wonderful, and they are miraculous, as they must be, because they are divinely given. How good of God to manifest Himself so clearly in our day as the God of miracles. I also praise God that He has broadened my vision to see that He has also blessed us by making all believers one—one with Him and one with one another. I have learned much from my brothers and sisters in other denominations, and I am thankful for them. I love them. This is another wonderful reality of the gospel. His church is universal, not sectarian. The bridegroom is not a polygamist. All glory, honor and praise be to Him, now and forever.

Appendix I

THE LETTER FROM RISTO SANTALA TO PAUL QUALBEN, M.D.

January 16

Dear Doctor Qualben,

For less than two weeks ago you had a lecture about the phenomenon of glossolalia in the Concordia Theological Seminary, Springfield, Illinois, and since the topic was dealt with reverently and scientifically I was impressed of your unbiased attitude. Among the examples given we heard also a tape when one and the same man spoke five different languages and sang a liturgical chant. According to the tape that I got of this lecture [you said that] "linguists that have analyzed many tapes of persons speaking in tongues have not found that any of them represent a known language or dialect." The aforesaid chant, however, shows all the signs of well-spoken Aramaic addenda. Since I have been preaching and teaching more than ten years in modern Hebrew in Jerusalem and since I have been used to medieval Rashi-Hebrew and Talmudic texts, I felt that it would good to notify you of the treasure you have in your hands.

The song mentioned above is a Hypodorian A-reciting tone, similar to Gregorian chant although its roots are pre-Gregorian monophonic plainsong. This type of singing traces back to first Christian hymns and ancient Temple service. The song has all the signs of professional musical work. Your lecture was partly on the first phrases of the chant, but I think that we got the whole song anyhow. See the ligatures and pneumatic notations. The whole song is well balanced beginning with the "clivis" and then with "virga subtri-punctum" followed by three beautiful phrases of "podatus" coming back to "virga subtripunctum" and closing with a peaceful "podatus."

The text is interesting and based mainly on Numbers 6:4, "The Lord bless thee." The name of God, which is never pronounced by a religious Jew is, however, departed to two synonyms of God, El and Jah, theologically a very interesting solution. The word "to bless" is repeated six times and always in strictly correct, grammatical forms (jevarechech, jevare-chech, vavarech, ve-jevarech, va-avaarech and avarech). The Hebrew equivalent in Numbers sounds: "Jevarechechaa." But as the object in this blessing is the "bride," in Aramaic "klaeea" and in Hebrew "kalaa," even the object is here in feminine form. This is already a master-work. The word Jah repeats six times; the Aramaic word, "Kaleea," bride, is in our song four times; the word "to hear," "shomeea" is twice; "hosheea," "to save" twice, "iish," "the man" twice.

The sentences are long and built with grammar. The pronunciation is of highest professional quality and has no American features whatsoever. In fact, I have been studying about eight years singing with a well known Jewish professor who taught also some Jewish cantors, and I must admit that this man glides over the words very distinctly and smoothly.

The song is divided to almost equal sections having typical Hebrew rhymes. Toward the end an "a" sound is added twice to words where it is not necessary because of the rhyme, but this is sometimes typical in Hebrew poetry. I shall write the song first as it sounds, and then using the Hebrew letters (again, no Hebrew typewriter, no Hebrew letters—sorry).

The translation is as follows: "...may the Lord God bless thee * O Man...of his * O Man "of-Him-He" bless the bride * that God shakes you, He hears and blesses the bride. * Behold He and he will bless completely as if in heaven * in order to save and God reveals His full power, * Thou hast made the Exalted One as if cursed by God and I shall bless the bride * the light of Messiah becomes wonderful. * He will answer, he saves. * I shall bless the bride with strong latter rain, He hears * raise (presumably corresponding to the Latin "sursum corda").

Our chant seems to belong to a kind of mystical bride-hymns with strong biblical emphasis. Its musical and linguistic level is high, but the theological concepts are still deeper. The song has some mystic features that cannot be invented without penetrating to ancient Jewish Cabbalist thinking.

a) The Man address is "iish an-da-ko-ho," a "man of-Him-He." Some Jewish scholars, like the Swedish Chief Rabbi Gottlieb Klein, have stated that the "forbidden name of God" (Shem Ha-mephorash) would be originally "ani ho," "ani hu" or in its Aramaic form "ana ho" or "ana ko"—the word used here is the best combination of this hidden name "an-da-ko-ho."

He is a "man" and He blesses the "bride," the congregation. Even Luther tried to solve the mystery of this name in
his book "Vom Schem Ha-Mophorash," a rather anti-Semitic
piece of literature.

b) The following subordinate sentence begins with
Aramaic word "are" "that," and the Messiah really "shakes
the heaven and the earth" (Haggai 2:6, Hebrews 12:26).

c) The Aramaic and Hebrew root, means in German
"denke" "sinne"—"think," or here, "behold," "be still."
Nowadays the Hebrew "dommi" means "to stand in attention." Even here every word is in logical form having a
deep message.

d) In this sentence only the word "pasha," presumably
"pashta" in Hebrew, has been pronounced so smoothly that
one does not hear almost the vanishing letter –, but in the
same sentence the word "to save," "Lehshiia" is pronounced
almost "loshia" as we do in our times.

e) The word "ashiita" is taken from the Psalm 110:1 and
is probably the only place where it appears in the Old Testament: "until I make Thy enemies a footstool for Thy feet."
Jesus quotes this verse as referring to Himself in Matthew
22:42–44. Here, however, our song relates it to Philippians
2:5–8. The word "oleh" means exactly "the Exalted One,"
"the raised one." He has been "made" "ka-shamda jah," "as
if God had destroyed him." The Hebrew expression about
Hebrew-Christians, "Mashummad" is of the same root. The
Exalted One became the first "Meshummad." He became

"cursed because of us"; "Christ redeemed us from the curse of the Law, having become a curse for us, for it is written, cursed is everyone who hangs on a tree" (Gal. 3:13).

g) The most interesting prophecy in this song is the promise of "the latter rain." If we follow the linguistic solutions in Semitic Bibles, in Deut. 32:2, Joel 3:23 or Hosea 6:3 we find the Hebrew word "Malkosh" in its former usage: lakish, lekisha, lakishin—and now lakishon. According to our Hebrew Bible, Joel 3:23 reads as follows: "He will give you the former rain for righteousness (or the 'teacher of righteousness' like in the Scrolls of the Dead sea and some Jewish rabbinic sources) and he will cause to come down for you the rain, the former rain and the latter rain." The former rain begins the rain season and the latter comes always just before the harvest, forming the flesh for the grain—in accord to this many Christians believe that there will be a short time of blessing before the second advent.

h) The conclusive "podatus" the peaceful "oleh" is a "sursum corda," "lift up your hearts," the finest ending this kind of chant could have.

SUMMA SUMMARUM: As we have seen, we meet in our chant profound musical expertness, good Hebrew pronunciation, old poetic type of language with pure rhymes, clear biblical message, which follows beautifully the music, and old mystic rabbinic ideas of God and "a Man" united, in accord to our Christian doctrine—everything in one and the same package, spoken as it seems to be in "glossolalia."

So would it please be possible to meet that 'package' in order to know about his spiritual, musical and theological background?

Sincerely yours,

Risto Santala

Appendix II

THE CHARGES

THE LIST OF charges presented by the elders to Pastor Dorpat on August 31 is as follows:

I. Unionism contrary to the Constitution and practices of the congregation and synod.

1. Participation in Full Gospel Business Men's Fellowship International meetings.

2. Participation in an interdenominational meeting in [a neighboring town].

3. Promotion of Charles P. Schmitt to speak at the college.

4. Support of selection of two Charismatics not on the clergy roster of the Lutheran Church—Missouri Synod to officiate at the funeral of a member of St. Mark's.

5. General disregard for the position of the congregation and the synod regarding fellowship and unionism:

   a. Admitted to encouragement of students to attend revival meetings of A. G. Dornfeld at [a neighboring town].

   b. Readiness to allow non-Lutherans to conduct worship at St. Mark's.

   c. Announcement in sermon of prayers with a Catholic priest.

d. Encouragement to CTC students to go to the Episcopal church to pray.

e. Opening of his home "prayer meetings" beyond Lutheran circles.

II. Doctrinal Concerns

1. Pastor Dorpat's "conclusions" concerning two "baptisms" cause members to question the validity and efficacy of the Sacrament of Holy Baptism when they hear or read Pastor Dorpat's statement that baptism with water is for justification and baptism with the Spirit is for sanctification.

2. Pastor Dorpat has exposed students to false doctrines by encouraging them to attend a "revival" meeting series of A. G. Dornfeld's at the Assembly of God church, May 2–9.

3. Pastor Dorpat has exposed students and members to the false doctrines of Charles P. Schmitt, whom he encouraged and promoted upon the student body and others who were invited to hear him.

4. Other questions arise concerning numerous other doctrines and emphases of Pastor Dorpat. They include:

a. The Law and the Gospel

b. Sufficiency of the Holy Scriptures

c. Doctrine of the Holy Spirit

III. Offensive Conduct

The congregation and elders, after repeated efforts, have failed to lead Pastor Dorpat to refrain from numerous practices which the congregation finds objectionable and, even if not wrong practices in themselves, are offensive. Therefore after persistent efforts to lead Pastor Dorpat from these types of conduct, the charge is brought of persistent offensive conduct.

Specific items of persistent offensive conduct include:

1. Failure to inform the elders and pastor when he came to [St. Mark's] that he was involved in the so-called Charismatic movement and spoke in tongues.

2. Frequent failure to communicate his plans and activities to the administrative pastor.

3. Distribution of questionable literature, as for example, the book *The Cross and the Switchblade*.

4. A growing lack of credibility and trust of Pastor Dorpat by a growing number of members within the congregation.

5. Widespread publicity brought about by Pastor Dorpat's activities associating the congregation with the so-called Charismatic movement and the baptism of the Holy Spirit.

6. Failure to abide by his statement before the elders and the circuit counselor that "he could work harmoniously with an administrative pastor who does not agree with the Charismatic movement." Illustrations of this include:

   a. Pastor Dorpat accuses Pastor Schmidt of having a closed mind to the Charismatic movement.

   b. Pastor Dorpat accuses Pastor Schmidt of false doctrine when presenting the traditional Missouri Synod approach and position to the Charismatic movement and speaking in tongues.

   c. Pastor Dorpat stated that he did not inform Pastor [Schmidt] of the continuation of "home prayer meetings" this summer because as Pastor Dorpat said: "I knew it would upset you."

7. Pastor Dorpat has been devious and secretive in dealing with the congregation, administrative pastor, and elders, especially in matters pertaining with the Charismatic movement.

8. On numerous occasions, Pastor Dorpat has "rundown" the Lutheran Church and its doctrinal position and practices.

9. Pastor Dorpat has provided the opportunity and climate for a "sect" (that is, a church within a church) to arise in the congregation by:

   a. Introducing weekly worship opportunities for periods of two or more hours per week without the knowledge and consent of the congregation.

   b. Continuing such prayer meetings in June and July. Pastor Dorpat has failed to "be especially sensitive to the congregational reaction to his home prayer meetings...and has failed to act 'so that his actions in these areas are above reproach by anyone.'" (Statement 3, St. Mark's Voters, June 7)

   c. Intentionally or non-intentionally, the "in-group" attending Pastor Dorpat's meetings has given the appearance to others that they have something special from God which others lack.

   d. Providing a second night of home meetings (Saturdays for two or more hours per week) for those who wanted a freer style of worship.

The document was signed by each of the eleven elders, dated August 29.

Appendix III

MY RESPONSE TO THE CHARGES

FIRST OF ALL, I appreciate the time you are all taking to come here. I believe you have the best interests of the kingdom of God at heart, although I also believe you are misled. But I do believe your intentions are honorable, and I praise God for that.

I also thank you for the chance to look at the charges that you have lined up. These were given to me last night after the voter's meeting. That's poor politics, but it's what a loving Christian brother would do. The political manipulator, of course, would have tried to get all the shock value out of the charges that he could. He would seek to ignore the dictates of the Lord in Matthew 18 to go to the brother alone with the concerns and lovingly admonish him in order to win him. He would rather seek to drop the accusations like a bomb with others present so that the opponent would feel threatened and would be led to react and in an emotional and frightened state to say things that he would not ordinarily say. Then, of course, these statements, too, could be used against him. But you have refused to act politically. Like Christian brothers, you have given these to me ahead of time that I might have a little time to look at them and prepare a response. Thank you. And know, concerning the specific charges:

I. Unionism

It is no secret that I do not agree with the Synod's stand on unionism. I don't believe the Synod itself believes with itself on this. I believe that the document of fellowship, which was adopted in New York, convincingly shows that we, as a synod, need to repent of a misuse of Scripture. I also believe that this subject should be studied in our elder's meetings and, if it can be shown from Scripture and the Confessions that I am wrong, I will surely repent and publicly acknowledge my mistakes.

While admitting my disagreement with what I believe is a false teaching of our church, I have not taught contrary to it and have not practiced contrary, except in one instance when I felt circumstances leading me to make an exception. That exception is point number two under the unionism category [of the charges], "participation in an interdenominational meeting in [a neighboring town]." I was asked to lead the opening prayer and I did. The building was, I had been told, a youth center. I had not been informed ahead of time that I would be called upon to lead the prayer, and I therefore felt it would have been a worse witness to Christ and my relationship with Him to refuse than to accept. Also, at the end of the meeting I was asked to help pray for the sick. This I stepped forward to do. However, I believe there were no requests for prayer at that time. If there were and I have forgotten, which isn't unlikely, then I plead guilty of praying for the sick.

I see number one and number five [of the charges] are related. I'm convinced that this also is not against the Lutheran position on unionism. If I understand this position, what is prohibited is the sharing of the platform, of participation in the service in a leadership capacity (as I did at [the interdenominational meeting]) with pastors or worship leaders of denominations not in fellowship with the Lutheran Church—Missouri Synod. I do not believe it is against our teaching on unionism simply to attend meetings of, for instance, the Full Gospel Business Men's Fellowship International or the Assembly of God churches. If this were the case, our seventh grade Sunday school classes would surely have been told that they were not to visit Catholic, Methodist, and other churches on Sunday morning as they have been doing this past summer. Also, when I was in prep school in Portland, one of our class assignments was to visit other churches. We were told that if we visited a non-Christian church, such as Christian Science, we should not participate in the worship, but if we visited a Christian church we should bow our heads in prayer and expect to be edified by the Word that was preached, discerning, of course, any false teaching by our own knowledge of the truth. I understand that this practice is a common procedure in all of the prep schools of our synod.

Worth mentioning, of course, is the example of our denomination's president, Dr. Preus, who preached in the White House in a Quaker chapel, while members of other denominations participated in the service, including a Presbyterian choir.

Number four under [the] unionism [charge] simply does not tell the facts. The facts in that case have been stated in elders meetings and now I have the chance to put them down in writing. I did not support the selection of two Charismatics to officiate at the funeral of a member of St Mark's. My first suggestion and only support, really, was that Pastor Schmidt should be contacted to have the service. When it became clear to me that the lady in question was not going to ask Pastor Schmidt, but that she wanted to have some one else preach at the service...(she mentioned two men, Charles Schmitt and Ray Kapp, who is a Lutheran), I suggested Kapp, for that reason, would be better than Schmitt. That was the extent of my involvement in that issue. I'm not saying that in the hurry of a long distance phone call and the shock of the news of the death of a close and loved friend I might not have said something wrong. But I did not do what number four [of the chares] says I did.

As far as the other "charges": They say that once you get into the machinery of being "defrocked" in the Missouri Synod, there's no way to get out. It is set up in such a way that, no matter what the charges are, the board of appeals of our synod invariably upholds the charges and denies the appeal of the individual being charged. I don't know if that is true or not, but that is what I have been told.

May I say that if these are charges that are being brought against me (I refer to numbers 3 and 5c, d, and e) then this particular case may make history in the Missouri Synod. The rest of the charges under unionism are, to my mind, laughable (except for 5b, which I don't understand). They would be laughable, that is, if they weren't false charges and therefore a breaking of the eighth commandment.

Take number three, the promotion of Charles Schmitt to speak at CTC. A review of the history of that particular occasion two years ago might be helpful. I believe that every church

GOD IS FAITHFUL

historian of note in our day sees the Charismatic movement [as a movement] to contend with, take note of, and be knowledgeable about. I believe that Concordia Teachers College and St. Mark's Lutheran Church should be aware of this Renewal movement. I had tried a number of times to introduce a discussion of the movement with the theology department of the college, both so that they would be aware of it and so that if I was off track in any way I could receive instruction from the Word to put me right. I highly respect the CTC theologians. These efforts were not successful. Therefore upon discovering that Charles Schmitt had some evenings available, we invited the theology department to our house in an informal atmosphere to talk about this Renewal that is spreading rapidly in the denominational churches in our day. I believe the statement of one man would, as ar s I could see, sum up the feeling of the majority of those at the meeting. He said, "I came here angry, but I am going away happy." I believe all of the men present recognized in Schmitt a genuine and loving Christian, who loves the Lord Jesus and who knows his Bible.

At that meeting in our home, I pointed out that Charles Schmitt had Thursday evening free and could speak at the college in Weller auditorium. We had tried hard to get another place, such as the...auditorium or one of the rooms at the civic center, but they were all taken. The only place left in town was Weller Auditorium. So we sought to get that in order that people might hear a speaker of this movement. I shared with the theologians and they suggested that, for the sake of peace in the congregation, I not be involved in presenting Mr. Schmitt. I reluctantly agreed. It was suggested that perhaps the ministerial association, of which I was the president, could sponsor Schmitt. I called a few members of the association and they were eager to cooperate. A panel to interview Schmitt and his wife was made up of two college professors, Dr. Erwin Kolb and Prof. Dan Cossens, and Father Petrus and the Rev. Ray Neutzman of the ministerial association. After the meeting, which was well-received by the vast majority, one of the professors of the college told Mr. Schmitt: "I don't know what you have, but whatever it is, I want it."

Since that time, there have been a number of speakers at Concordia, including a Jewish rabbi, a spokesman for the Gay Liberation movement, and others. There have also been other speakers sponsored by the ministerial association. To say that the scheduling of and listening to a speaker is unionism is simply ridiculous.

As far as 5c, "the announcement in a sermon of prayers with a Catholic priest": in that same sermon I pointed out that this was at Concordia Seminary, that it was not in a worship service, and that it was in a Lutheran setting and that this priest simply wanted to thank and praise God with someone because he had finally come to know Jesus as Savior and Lord! To call that unionism, offensive, and a sin, is nothing short of twisting the intentions of God's Word. And the very idea of putting this down here as a charge would indicate to me and, I believe, to any fair-minded evangelical Christian, a spirit of deceit and sinful judging. Rather than listing this as a charge, it would seem to me to be the duty of the pastors and the elders of St. Mark's to point out the beauty of such an occurrence and to correct the false interpretations of such a self-righteous, judging attitude. If angels in heaven rejoice over one sinner who repents, why shouldn't we? The person who would judge that such a godly thing was a sin is, as Jesus would say, in danger of being judged.

Concerning 5d: "Encouragement of CTC students to go to the Episcopal Church to pray." This might just be the one charge that would get the board of appeals in such a good mood from the humor of it that the board would make the historical decision that was mentioned earlier. Pardon me for being sarcastic, but it is beyond me why either [charges] d or c should ever be mentioned as a charge—d, the encouragement too pray, and c, the encouragement for non-Lutherans to come to a Lutheran service!

Perhaps some background for 5d would be in place. I don't remember "encouraging students to go the Episcopal church to pray." I remember mentioning that they did and, perhaps, saying that I thought it was a good idea, and I still do. I think I would encourage anyone to go there to pray when our church is locked. The students went there last year because that church was open all night for that specific purpose. While I don't know how many students went to drink and pet and see x-rated movies, these students went to the Episcopal church to pray. Praise God!

II. Doctrinal Concerns

1. Pastor Dorpat's "conclusions" concerning two "baptisms" cause members to question the validity and efficacy of the sacrament of Holy Baptism when they hear or read Pastor Dorpat's statement that baptism with water is for justification and baptism with the Holy Spirit is for sanctification.

It might come as a surprise to you that that is the traditional position of our synod. I am preparing a paper on the misconceptions concerning the Charismatic movement, the baptism of the Holy Spirit, and the gift of tongues. I hope to have it ready this week and will be glad to give it to you and as many theologians as I can, for your and their critical study. I would like to read an excerpt from page four of that paper:

> Some years ago in *The Lutheran Witness* column "What's the Answer?" this question was asked: "How do water baptism and the baptism of the Holy Spirit differ from one another?" *The Witness* gave this answer: "While the Holy Spirit is inseparably associated with water baptism, by which he works the new birth (John 3:5–6, Titus 3:5), the baptism of the Spirit is not a sacrament, but a special bestowal of spiritual gifts on the faithful. Joel and John the Baptist foretold the baptism of the Spirit (Joel 2:28–29; Matt. 3:11), and Jesus alluded to it (John 7:37–39). Fulfillment of it occurred in Jerusalem (Acts 2:1–4), Caesarea (Acts 10:44–48), Ephesus (Acts 19:1–6), and Corinth (1 Cor. 12:11). A listing of such spiritual gifts is recorded in Romans 12:6–8 and 1 Cor. 12:11. He could bestow them now, but there is no promise to that effect. Certainly the possession of special spiritual gifts by modern Christians cannot be an indispensable mark of the true church, since there are false signs. (See Matthew 24:24 and 2 Thessalonians 2:8–100.) Sinners are saved by the Gospel, not by signs and wonders.

In speaking against the proposition that the outpouring of the Spirit on the disciples at Pentecost was a means of grace, a part of the "salvation history" (as proposed by Pastor Schmidt in his Pentecost sermon) "needed to put them into complete possession of the remission of sins and membership in the kingdom," Dr. Francis Pieper, in "Christian Dogmatics" (Vol.

III, Page 289) says: "But in point of fact, the outpouring of the Holy Ghost on the Day of Pentecost had the purpose of equipping the disciples for their calling as witnesses of Christ in the world: 'But you shall receive power after that the Holy Ghost is come upon you; and ye shall be witnesses unto me in Jerusalem, and in all Judea, and in Samaria, and unto the uttermost parts of the earth'" (Acts 1:8, KJV).[1]

In a footnote to the above, Pieper then points out that there are differences in the use of the word *baptism* in the Bible. There are different "baptisms," as the author of the letter to the Hebrews says in chapter six, verse two: "Of the doctrine of baptisms." There is, as the Nicene Creed states it: "One baptism for the remission of sins." I believe that is the "one baptism" that Paul refers to in Ephesians 4:5. That baptism is baptism in water in the name of the triune God. Pieper's footnote says "Lutheran theologians accordingly distinguish 'baptismus flaminis' or the outpouring of the special gifts of the Holy Spirit (Acts 1:5), from 'baptismus fluminis,' or the baptism with water, which is a sacrament for the remission of sins."

Pieper lists as the reference for his teaching on these different baptisms Johann Andreas Quenstedt, called by the *Lutheran Cyclopedia*, the "bookkeeper of Lutheran ortho-doxy" and his work that is quoted is described as "a standard of Lutheran orthodoxy."

As far as number two under "Doctrinal Concerns" is concerned, I believe that is a matter for the college. In their letter of sincere thanks and commendation to me for my ministry to the college students, no mention is made of disapproval of the attendance of the students at such meetings. I believe that Pastor Dornfeld is a fine man. Besides, he is of Lutheran back-ground and persuasion.

I would appreciate being informed of any bad results among those who attended the meeting which the charges say I promoted. I am convinced that if anyone did go to hear him, they would have been edified and blessed. I believe I could bring you letters by the dozen, and perhaps by the million if we would go beyond CTC, that would express the reality of changed lives and dedication to Christ, of zeal for witnessing to His love and renewed understanding of the Lutheran teachings concerning grace alone, faith alone, scriptures alone, that have been gained through the ministry of men like Pastor Dornfeld.

The same is true of number three.

Concerning number four, questions concerning other doctrines: The Law and the Gospel—if I have mixed them, I would appreciate documentation of this on the basis of the Word, and I would gladly recant and repent if, on that basis, I was convinced that I had erred. I'm reminded of a story concerning Dr. Luther, when he once left the pulpit in deep disgust with himself. He spit on his robe and said to himself, "What a terrible sermon." Then he sat down and had a glass of beer, leaving the sermon in the hands of the Holy Spirit who works the miracle of faith. I have often left the pulpit feeling that I had done a very inadequate job of preaching. I have often felt that I had done a very good job too.

I believe far worse than mixing law and gospel is the use of the law as a club to tear down and destroy. I believe that this has been going on for some time in elder's meetings and is evidenced in the many false accusations of these charges.

Sufficiency of the Holy Scriptures? I love God's Word.

Doctrine of the Holy Spirit? I believe I am orthodox on

all of these. If there are some specific charges based on Scripture that would convince me that I have preached falsehood, I would be glad to recant in dust and ashes. I believe the listing of them as they are here again will only encourage more rumor and gossip and do a disservice to the board of elders and this congregation.

III. Offensive Conduct

1. Failure to inform the Elders and Pastor when he came to St. Mark's that he was involved in the so-called "Charismatic movement" and spoke in "tongues."*

I believe you will understand why I didn't share this right away. I believe that it was God who led me on this course of action. I followed this general rule (after much prayer about it): I would not share my experience unless I was asked. Those with whom I shared this, including my father and other counselors that I respected, thought it was a good rule to follow. The rationale behind this course of action was, I believe, one of love. I did not want to push people and cause them to wrestle with something that appeared strange and unusual. But if they would ask, I would be glad to share with them and satisfy their interest. I did mention in a sermon to the congregation that I had attended a Charismatic conference in Minneapolis...and it was after that that I shared my experience with Pastor Heidemann. He urged me to share it with the circuit pastoral conference, and, in turn, he also shared with me some of his experiences with the Holy Spirit.

I am aware of the deceitfulness of my own flesh and

---

* Before we came to Centerville, we did share this with the senior pastor, Dr. Heidemann.

recognize that my motive in not sharing my experience so readily could have been selfishly motivated on the fear of such a meeting as this. If this was, indeed the case, although I don't believe it was, and if my decision was unwise, I apologize. I repeat, I believe it was God's will for me. If it wasn't God's will but rather my own, I ask your forgiveness.

2. Frequent failure to communicate his plans and activities to the administrative pastor.

When I first came to St. Mark's as assistant pastor, Dr. Heidemann made it very clear that I was a pastor, one of the pastors of St. Mark's. I was told that we would share the burden of the ministry here as equally as possible. I believe that this arrangement was a reality to such an extent that when the elders met to decide upon the title of the pastor we would be calling they didn't know that Pastor Heidemann's call read that he was head pastor and my call read that I was assistant pastor.

When we changed the titles after Dr. Heidemann left to pastor and administrative pastor, there was concern expressed in the voter's meeting that someone should have the responsibility for leadership. I then drew up some guidelines which spelled out what I felt was the situation in the office of the ministry at St. Mark's during the joint ministry of Pastor Heidemann and myself and which also reflected the intentions of the elders and voters. Pastor Heidemann, when hearing of this action, mentioned that it should have been done years ago.

It was my understanding that the adoption of the guidelines established a team ministry, a co-pastor relationship, with the administrative pastor as the leader of the team and that my original call as assistant pastor had therefore been dropped and the new guidelines superseded that original call. I still feel that is the case. The reason I didn't raise any objections in the elder's meeting that discussed my call was that I feel this is not the issue at stake in the present controversy. I believe that this issue of my call is being used as a political tactic to dodge the real issue, which is: the Charismatic movement and the biblical basis of the same. If I am wrong, please forgive me.

I feel the aforementioned discussion in the voter's assembly reflected the realization of the voters that the change of title was indeed a change of the call from assistant pastor to a co-pastor arrangement.

Those guidelines that the voters adopted spell out a co-pastorate of pastors working together, making decisions together, responsible together, sharing the burdens of the office under the leadership of the administrative pastor, but not under his dictatorial rule as boss. I believe this is the New Testament way. I don't know of any place in the New Testament where you have a one-man leadership. Elders (pastors, teachers, overseers, etc) are always spoken of in the plural, as Paul says of himself and Apollos in 1 Corinthians 3:8 that they are "one" (KJV)!

Now, as far as my failure to communicate my plans and activities to the administrative pastor: I presume this is referring to the meetings that were held on Thursday evenings in our home. As soon as Pastor Schmidt arrived, I encouraged him again and again to attend those meetings. For some reason, he did not accept our invitation.

The guidelines say, "as the two pastors work together they may find that a clearer division of duties will be desirable depending upon the talents and aptitudes of the men. If such a division of duties is agreed upon, that pastor who assumes a given area of leadership (such as stewardship, education, organization, Bible class, etc.) shall be primarily responsible for that area." The area of ministry to the college students had been assigned to me from the beginning, and I felt I was responsible for it and felt I shared as much as should have with the administrative pastor. If I was wrong and the elders would like me to share a detailed account of each of my days of ministry, I will be glad to do that. I do not believe that the guidelines at all require this, however. I also do not believe that this is an issue. If it will keep harmony in the church and if we are able to get at the issue of what the Bible says, then I would be glad to take the title of office boy or doorkeeper. The Gentiles are concerned about titles.

3. The distribution of questionable literature; as for example, the book, *The Cross and the Switchblade*.

To this I plead guilty. I believe *The Cross and the Switchblade* is one of the finest Christian books of our day. I believe it has been instrumental in causing many to examine the claims of Christ in His Word and ultimately to turn to Him as Savior and Lord. It was assigned as a textbook in one of the college courses last year.

4. A growing lack of credibility and trust of Pastor Dorpat by a growing number of members within the congregation.

Here permit me to quote an article from "The Message of the Cross" magazine:

> There is much discussion about tongues these days. We are living in days of two great tongues movements. Many are talking about tongues. But it seems very clear that one worldwide tongues movement must surely be of the Devil. It brings division; it causes churches to break up,

pastors to lose their positions, and others to lose their effectiveness. Certainly it ought to be condemned. This tongues movement is not the one described in 1 Cor. 12 and 14, where the early church, filled with the Holy Spirit, were extolling and praising God in languages they had not learned. The Devil's tongues movement is described in James 3: "So the tongue is a little member and boasts of great things.... The tongue is an unrighteous world among our members, staining the whole body, setting on fire the cycle of nature, and set on fire by hell. It is this manifestation that splits churches, slanders pastors and other workers, makes workers ineffective, gladdens the devil and his servants and fills hell. Gossiping, back-biting, tale bearing, criticism is the tongues movement of the day. We need a great return to repentance. We especially need to repent of the sins of the tongue. This unruly member must be brought under the dominion of the Holy Spirit. All of this is promised and is possible through the redemption of the Lord Jesus Christ.

In the guidelines drawn up by the United Presbyterian Church under the title: "For ministers who have not had neo-Pentecostal experiences" is this second directive: "Seek first-hand knowledge of what New Pentecostalism means to those who have experienced it. Avoid a judgment until this first hand knowledge is obtained."

Morton Kelsey in his book *Tongues Speaking* points out that the Charismatic Renewal can be divisive when either side becomes militant, that is, when those who have not had neo-Pentecostal experiences seek to deny any efficacy or worth to them and, in fact, speak or campaign against them.[2]

Dr. E. V. Kalin of Concordia Seminary, St. Louis, speaking

to the pastoral conference…said: "Isn't it divisive? Of course it can be. So can any gift of God. If it is misused or if it is treated with contempt by those who do not possess it. We sometimes act as if something cannot possibly be right and Christian and Lutheran and God-pleasing if we have never done it before."

I believe all of us need to examine ourselves and need to repent if we have thought, spoken, or acted wrongly.

Far from seeking to make this experience of the baptism of the Holy Spirit normative for all Christians, I have been accused of being too quiet—secretive, even.

On the other hand, I feel that God's Word has been mostly ignored by the accusers in the present case. In fact, the board of elder's meetings have themselves become an instrument of gossip, which is one of the Devil's greatest tools to divide people and bring dishonor to the church. The critical, judging spirit is the spirit of the accuser, Satan.

Let me clarify. In Matthew 18 we have the clear procedure for handling offenses by a brother. Very rarely has this procedure been followed in these last months. I have been told that there are numerous people who have found my involvement in the Charismatic movement offensive. But they have not come to talk to me, and I have not been given their names that any offense that might have been taken might be removed. If they are unwilling to come to me and unwilling for me to come to them, then they should repent of the sin of gossip and judging. I believe the failure to follow this biblical procedure, accompanied with the negative tone of the guidelines and the repeated negative preaching by Pastor Schmidt against the Charismatic movement and the holy, biblical gifts of the Spirit, has increased the problem and has proven to be divisive.

Now, to clarify concerning the board of elders meetings being themselves instruments of gossip. One member of our church told me in an off-hand remark that the wife of one of the elders had told her that Pastor Dorpat has even been caught in telling a lie! In the light of the fact that there has been an apparent refusal to act upon biblical lines and seek to stop judging and gossip, I ask the question: who is being divisive?

5. Widespread publicity brought about by Pastor Dorpat's activities associating the congregation with the so-called Charismatic movement and the baptism with the Holy Spirit.

To that, I can only say praise God.

6. Failure to abide by his statement before the Elders and the circuit Counselor that he "could work harmoniously with an administrative pastor who does not agree with the Charismatic movement."

I believe that I can work harmoniously with such an administrative pastor. I am fully willing to accept him and his gifts, but he apparently finds it impossible to accept me and my gifts. I have not been bringing in accusations and wasting the time of the elders with them. When accusations have been brought to elder's meeting, I have tried to defend myself against them and have, at times, felt threatened and perhaps said things I shouldn't have. For that I am deeply sorry, but I think it should be noted that I have not been the one who has come in with all sorts of prepared statements designed to accuse and shock. Again to quote Dr. Kalin:

> If we seek to keep from excluding or isolating someone
> by whether he does or does not have a certain gift

or pattern of worship, or style of Christian life, then we are on the way to being the catholic, ecumenical, edifying, lively community we are meant to be.

Let's look at specific illustrations:

"Pastor Dorpat accuses Pastor Schmidt of having a closed mind about the Charismatic movement. I believe this fits in with the next statement: "Pastor Dorpat accuses Pastor Schmidt of false doctrine when presenting the traditional Missouri Synod approach to and position on the Charismatic movement and speaking in tongues." Forgive me if this sounds blunt and harsh, but I believe Pastor Schmidt doesn't have any idea of what the traditional Missouri approach is. I believe that is apparent in the content of objection number one under "Doctrinal Concerns" about the baptism of the Holy Spirit. It is also true concerning his teaching on the gift of tongues. What Pastor Schmidt presented on the gift of tongues in his sermon on the subject were direct quotations from a book by the Southern Baptists. It may not be the worst book published on glossolalia, but the section written by Frank Stagg, entitled "Glossolalia in the New Testament," and from which pastor Schmidt took his quotations is, in my opinion, one of the worst. The logic and twisting of scripture is indefensible, and I am ready to sit down with any number of theologians and discuss the chapter point by point with the Bible at hand. At any rate, the teaching of that sermon was from one Southern Baptist and not from a Lutheran theologian.

I believe that the following is the issue in this case: what does the Bible say? That is what we should be discussing. I believe that the charges against me are a device to get off this basic question. I will not stand for that. I will be a thorn in the side of you, Pastor Schmidt, and you, the board of elders, and of this congregation until we get into the Scriptures and see what they have to say. This other catalogue of charges is a waste of time and (forgive me if I am wrong, I feel we must be honest with one another) mostly a twisting of the truth or an out and out lie.

I believe Pastor Schmidt's closed mind to the Charismatic movement has been amply displayed in his sermons on this issue, which were not only unbiblical, but anti-biblical in that they spoke against what the Bible calls a gift of the Holy Spirit. I also believe that the selection of the materials that Pastor Schmidt chose to present to the elders in what he called his Bible class—but what I was told was to be a mutually worked-out Bible class—also shows this closed mind. For instance, in the first class, after much urging on my part, we did use my outline on 1 Corinthians 12–14, but we never finished it. We never got to the many positive things Paul said about the gift of tongues that were a part of his own ministry and prayer life—like "I thank God I speak in tongues more than all of you!" (1 Cor. 14:18).

The next Sunday we listened to the reading of an article from the Concordia Theological Monthly (CTM). Without discussing it with me, Pastor Schmidt read the one article from the CTM which was the most out-of-date, negative, and irrationally emotional. He stated that this was the stand of our synod without mentioning that since that article was written there have been two more in the CTM that were very positive about the movement, as were other articles in periodicals such as *The Lutheran Forum* and *Advance Magazine*. To take the one outdated article and call it the stance of the Synod is, to my mind—and forgive me if I'm wrong—not only closed-minded but, it appears to me, devious.

Next, Pastor Schmidt read from Dr. Mayer's excellent book *The Religious Bodies of America*. He read the section that reveal the errors (according to Lutheran dogma) of the Pentecostal churches, beliefs that I also believe are in error. By reading the objections of classical Pentecostalism, it seems to me that Pastor Schmidt implied a kind of guilt by association and, in effect, sought to bring condemnation upon a movement…and upon a person, me…I don't know if this was intentional, but what it amounts to is—again forgive me if I am wrong—slander.

As far as not informing Pastor Schmidt about our home prayer meetings, I believe he knew all about them. Furthermore, they were on my free time and I was trying to be sensitive to the feelings of some in the congregation by agreeing (and going beyond the requirements of Scripture, 1 Corinthians 14:39–40) to not be free in the expression of the gifts of the Spirit in the meetings, thus removing anything that could possibly be objectionable. I believe that I have followed the guidelines explicitly in spirit and in the letter. I have the assurance from others, including President Janzow, that this was the meaning of the guidelines. They did not forbid meetings. As soon as I was told by the board of elders to stop the meetings, though the guidelines do not indicate that I should, we did stop them.

7. Pastor Dorpat has been devious and secretive in dealing with the congregation, administrative pastor and elders, especially in matters pertaining with the Charismatic movement.

I do not believe I have been devious. My intentions were to be loving. I have not wanted to cause people trouble and therefore I have not publicized my involvement. As I have said before, I have gone with the principle of answering when asked.

8. On numerous occasions Pastor Dorpat has "run down" the Lutheran church and its doctrinal positions and practices.

I believe I have preached the Word of God. If I have not, I would appreciate being told specifics, at which time I would recant and repent publicly and privately, or both, if I am convinced from God's Word that I have taught falsely.

9. Pastor Dorpat has provided the opportunity and climate for a church within the church by introducing weekly worship opportunities for periods of two or more hours per week without the knowledge and consent of the congregation.

In sermons, (long before Pastor Schmidt was here) I mentioned our Thursday evening prayer meetings and my involvement in the Charismatic movement when I first got here and no one seemed to be offended by those referrals. At least, no one came to talk to me about them.

Concerning "introducing weekly worship opportunities for periods of two or more hours per week without the knowledge and consent of the congregation." Introducing them? I didn't. The students were sent to me by the dean of the chapel and in my capacity of pastor concerned for the spiritual life of the students and CTC, I provided our home as a place for them to meet. You all know this, and I don't understand why this is down on the list at all. Again, I can only deduce this as an example of the devious nature of these charges. I was asked by the college to provide this service, and it was under the college's authority that they were conducted. During the time when there was some gossip on the campus about them, I talked informally with some of the professors, notably the dean of students and the dean of the chapel, whether they should be stopped. They assured me that that would not be necessary.

I believe my actions concerning these prayer meetings have been completely above reproach. My conscience is clear concerning them. It may be of interest to you to know that they will continue in this school year. They will be student-led by the same students that led them in our home. They will be in the homes of the various professors who might volunteer to host them.

Concerning "…. Continuing such prayer meetings in June and July, Pastor Dorpat has failed to especially be sensitive to congregational reaction to his home prayer meetings…. and has failed to act 'so that his actions in these areas are above reproach by any one'" (Statement 3 St. Mark's voters, June 7).

The credibility gap that was mentioned in the minutes of our elder's meetings, as I remember, concerned the continuation of the summer meetings. The charge was made that I continued them without the approval and the knowledge of the college administration. I believe that pastor Schmidt will now be able to close that gap because President Janzow has informed him personally that the meetings were conducted with both the knowledge and the approval of president Janzow.

Concerning "… providing a second night of home meetings (Saturdays for two or more hours per week for those who wanted a freer style of worship)." I believe that the Saturday evening meetings have also been carried on out of love. Again, the issue is the Charismatic movement and the gifts of the Spirit. If the movement is not valid and the Bible says they are not valid, then, of course, we would have no reason to have Saturday evening meetings. But if they are valid and if they are used to build up the body of Christ—and they are—then it would seem to me that those who have been blessed with these gifts ought to meet together in order to build one another up. But until the church is educated and understands what the Bible teaches concerning the gifts, they probably shouldn't be too open in the expression of their gifts. About that I may be wrong. They are open in other churches, such as the Catholic church, and in churches of other denominations around the country, and they don't seem to be causing the trouble that we are experiencing here. However, I can see where, out of love, they would want to meet privately and not invite anyone who might take offense.

Concerning, "intentionally or non-intentionally the 'in group' attending pastor Dorpat's meetings has given the appearance to others that they have something special from God which others lack." We all have different "special" gifts, talents and abilities from God that others do not have. Why should that divide us? Why should that cause envy, jealousy, and gossip?

I believe that it might be premature to ask anyone to resign because this situation has been handled so poorly, because gossip has not been stopped, because the Word of God has not been the focus of our attention, and because we have not followed the directives of our Lord in Matthew 18.

I would think that if anyone has refused to follow Matthew 18 and to come to me with their concerns before presenting them to others; or has refused to encourage others to come to me that the situation might be cleared up and the gossip stopped; or if they have twisted the Scripture to say what it does not say; or if they have sought to throw up smoke screens and to attack people instead of talking about the issues, coming together as brothers and sisters to see what the Bible says about the Baptism of the Holy Spirit and about tongues and being willing to listen to one another, then I believe that repentance and a retraction and an apology would be in order. And if the repentance and retraction does not come, then I believe resignations would be in order.

I guess you can sense a certain difference of opinion between Pastor Schmidt and myself. I believe that this can be cleared up. I do not hold ill-will toward Pastor Schmidt. I am often tempted to, but then I remember my sinfulness and I think of Jesus' love and forgiveness and I find the ability to forgive and to love, not in myself, but in Him who lives in me. I would suggest that the proposal a respected brother in the ministry made to both of us be followed. That is, that we sit down with a brother we both respect and hash out our differences. I feel that before we would do that, that we both repent of any sins that we have committed against one another, real or imagined, and that we shake hands and speak words of forgiveness to one another. I would suggest that, because of his nearness to us, President Niedner be asked to be the referee.

Concerning the present issues about the Charismatic movement and my involvement in the same:

1. It should be studied on the basis of Scripture, involving not only those who have not had neo-Pentecostal experiences, but also those who have.

2. Any who take offense at my involvement in the Renewal should follow the procedure in Scripture of coming to me and talking about it (Matt. 18:15–17).

3. In the mean time, to guard against "church within the church," opportunities should be officially be available for prayer meetings, Bible study meetings, song meetings on the New Testament pattern, etc., openly, in the church basement or in homes, in order that all might freely attend or not attend.

Appendix IV

MY FAREWELL LETTER
TO THE CONGREGATION

Dear member of St. Mark's,

This letter, written with a heavy heart, is to announce to you my resignation from the pastorate of St. Mark's Lutheran Church. Following are some of my reasons and concerns, which I would ask you to read prayerfully.

I first of all would like to apologize to any and all of the members of St. Mark's for any failure in my ministry here. I know there have been many. I have been far from a perfect pastor. I'm sure there were calls I should have made, things I should have done differently, words I should have left unsaid, shortcomings I have displayed, and time I have misspent. If my sins have been hidden to others, they have been only too obvious to me. I ask you to forgive me.

On the other hand I am still convinced that I have been teaching, preaching, and believing in strict accord with Scripture and the Lutheran Confessions. I am very sorry that at the special voter's meeting on October 12 concerns were brought up and spelled out, which I had previously answered satisfactorily. The reiteration of those concerns, plus all the other talk that undoubtedly has been going on, has placed me in the unfortunate position, if I would stay at St. Mark's, of having to put all my effort and time into explanations and apologies, doctrinal discussions, and attempts at meeting antagonisms. I wouldn't have any time left to really help lead the church in moving on with the building of the kingdom.

When you are playing football and you are penalized ten yards, you are at a big disadvantage. Before you can even think of making any further advance down the field, you have to battle like everything just to get back to the original line of scrimmage. I believe that is how it would be for me at St. Mark's, and therefore I am now seeking to serve the church and our Lord elsewhere where such obstacles are not present.

I am also aware that even if we could each sit down, face-to-face, and talk about the issues that are involved in the present controversy, the feelings run so deeply and there has been so much (in my mind) misinformation that the task of seeking reconciliation is almost insurmountable.

I know that many of our members have hard feelings toward me. They feel that I have been the cause of this "dark hour" that has come upon our congregation. They feel that I have been misled down a wrong path. Some have said worse things. My great regret in having to resign is that I cannot sit down with these people and take time to talk out these feelings. The scriptures say that "He who believes and is baptized will be saved" (Mark 16:16, RSV), and that "he who believes in the Son has eternal life" (John 3:36, RSV). I believe in Christ Jesus as my Savior from sin and [as] the Lord of my life. I know I am a child of God, and I know that many if not all the members who have these feelings are also believers in Jesus and children of God. That being the case, we are brothers and sisters, and I am sure that with time and with the power of the gospel of forgiveness, reconciliation could be accomplished. However, some, I am sure, would not be willing to talk at this time. Others are so angry that if they did talk, they wouldn't be willing to listen. Again, I am sure there is some basis for these feelings. I know that I have not been a perfect pastor, and I ask your forgiveness.

On the other hand, I believe (and I realize that I could be wrong) many of these feelings are based on rumor and hearsay. It isn't by accident that Scripture says that the tongue is the most wicked member of the body and capable of doing the greatest harm to the kingdom. I hope and pray that we have gone at least a little way toward learning not to draw conclusions and make judgments on the basis of rumor and second- or third-hand information. If justice is to be done and reputations guarded, we must act and speak only on first-hand knowledge. Even with first-hand knowledge, if it is of a nature that might harm anyone, it should be handled according to the dictates of Scripture (Matthew 18:15–17 and the eighth commandment). Perhaps the Word of God in Hosea 5:15–6:3 are applicable to us all (God is speaking):

> I will return again to my place, until they acknowledge their guilt and seek my face, and in their distress they seek me, saying, "Come, let us return to the LORD; for he has torn, that he may heal us; he has stricken, and he will bind us up. After two days he will revive us; on the third day he will raise us up, that we may live before him. Let us know, let us press on to know the Lord; his going forth is sure as the dawn; he will come to us as the showers, as the spring rains water the earth.

As we all at St. Mark's mutually repent and seek the Lord, healing will come and, perhaps, through this trial and chastisement of the Lord, an even greater and more dedicated membership.

Now, permit me to make something clear. I feel the organized Christian church is in bad shape. There are cutbacks in mission outreach in almost all the major denominations, including our Lutheran church. In a time of great prosperity, such as the world has never before known, with the greatest tools of all time at our disposal, including mass and swift transportation, instant communication and the financial resources to send out the laborers, we are failing to reach the world for Christ. The church is called to be more than a group of people concerned about getting themselves saved. The church is called to be an army of people who *are* saved through faith in Jesus Christ, know it by God's grace, and are being equipped to reach out to save others. The "equipment" to accomplish that is the power of the Holy Spirit. Can any one deny that the evidence of that power is often lacking in the church? When the average church member can, as a matter of course, with no qualms of conscience, spend more money on luxuries than he gives to spread the Gospel or feed the hungry, when he has no real desire to meditate on the Word of God or pray with any regularity, when he is unwilling and/or unable to witness to his faith, then something is wrong.

In my eight years of contact with the Charismatic Renewal (two years of study and six years of involvement), I have come to be convinced that God is pouring out His Spirit in a very convincing way to renew His church. Surely mistakes are made, sins go on, there is not always doctrinal purity by Lutheran standards, but there also is [with the Renewal] a vitality, a willingness and a power to proclaim Christ only with joy and with conviction that is lacking in the organized church. And there are results! Lives are being changed. People by the millions are coming to Christ. I plead with you to be open to what God is doing in our day.

As long as I am wound up and still running, there are a few more concerns that I would like to bring to your attention.

Some will ask why I waited until now to resign. You may believe me or not, but the main reason I have not resigned before this is that every time I got on my knees to pray about it the answer seemed to be "no." From a human point of view, the main reason I refused was that I did not believe the congregation was facing the issues. I felt that if I resigned without first attempting to explain my position and seek to correct the rumors I would be in fact admitting that the rumors were true. I know firsthand that they are false.

Some will also still ask why I didn't tell the members of the church about my experience with the Holy Spirit before I came to St. Mark's. I expressed myself on this at the October 12 voter's meeting, but would like to make it clear to all the members, so permit me to quote what I said at that meeting:

> I would like to explain why I didn't share my experience with the fullness of the Holy Spirit before I came to St. Mark's Lutheran Church. I will not take the time to tell you what happened in my life six years ago. I have included that in an appendix of a paper I have written on some of the issues involved in the Charismatic movement and there are copies of that available for you to have. At that time I was eager to share this

(my experience) with people, but after counseling with my peers in the ministry, my circuit counselor and my brother (they advised me not to be too open), I decided that I would not share my experience with others unless they asked. I really felt that this was, at least for the time being, the procedure that God wanted me to follow. This is the procedure that I followed when I came to Centerville. I have been told that many feel this was deceitful land underhanded. But I ask you, if you had received the gift of tongues would you go and tell everyone? Would you tell everyone, especially when your circuit counselor, your close friends, and as far as I believe, God Himself, advised you against it?

I would also like to clarify a statement that I was told I made at the October 12 voter's meeting. I am told I said that "no one" has come to see me. If I said that (it is not down on my written statement and was therefore an off-hand remark) I apologize. I was mistaken. A few did come to see me before the voter's meeting. Many more have come since that meeting. I truly appreciate that. As President Niedner said in last Sunday's sermon, we must communicate.

There is one more item I would like to mention in this letter. St. Mark's has always had the problem of the differences in background, training, and oratorical abilities between the college professors and the townspeople. I don't suppose there was ever a meeting that demonstrated that difference more convincingly than the October 12 meeting. Almost everyone who spoke was a college professional. Many townspeople have long had the feeling that "the college is taking over and running our church." A look at the make-up of the boards and committees of the congregation would indicate that this is simply not true, even if it sometimes appears so from the talks in the meetings. The very fact that I am resigning would indicate that what is said in the meetings doesn't necessarily dictate what final action is taken [the professors had kindly and strongly spoken in my favor]. At any rate, no matter what our differences, we have one vital uniting factor: we are all one in Christ. I am sure that if all parties would seek God's will, pray for one another, communicate with one another, and forgive one another as they have been forgiven through the blood of Christ, there would be no need for feelings of separation and division.

My family and I will always remember the many friends we have made at St. Mark's. If any of you have questions or are holding grudges, please come and see us and talk. We pray that through the grace of God, St. Mark's may become the kind of community of God's people that can accept one another, love one another, and harmoniously apply the healing balm of the gospel to the great needs existing in our community and in the world at large.

Sincerely, in Christ,

—D. M. DORPAT

Appendix V

LUTHER ON THE SPIRIT
AND HIS GIFTS

MARTIN LUTHER, THE primary leader of the Reformation, which freed sixteenth-century Western society from the oppressive grip of a papacy that had wandered from the ancient truths of the gospel of salvation in Jesus Christ, was not an enemy of the charismatic gifts of the Spirit. Following are a few of his comments on the Spirit and His gifts:

I. "If the office of teaching be entrusted to anyone, then everything accomplished by the Word in the church is entrusted, that is, the office of baptizing, consecrating, binding, loosing, praying and judging doctrine. Inasmuch as the office of preaching is the greatest of all and certainly is apostolic, it becomes the foundation for all other functions, which are built upon it, such as the offices of teachers, prophets, governing (the church), speaking with tongues, the gifts of healing and helping, as Paul directs in 1 Cor. 12:28."[1]

II. (Commenting on Isaiah 12:2–3: "The Lord God is my Strength and my Song.") "The strength is my strength, that is, my kingdom, my house, the victorious power through which I have my enemies under my feet and shall trample the serpent underfoot, etc. The Song is my song, my psalm, the subject matter of my psalm and song. I have no one to sing and chant about but Christ, in him alone I have everything. Him alone I proclaim, in Him alone I glory for he has become my salvation, that is, my victory. For thus the word 'salvation' is often used in the Scriptures for 'victory.' Our victory is Christ, and when we boast of Christ we shall win!

"Satan and the ungodly hear the Word of God not willingly but unwilling, yet this Word consoles and lifts up the godly who are alarmed either in the hour of death or in want and misfortune....Satan is not thrown out by means of plans made by the flesh, but by the means of studying the Word of God.

"With joy will you draw water from the wells of salvation. After the Word of the Gospel has been preached and the voice of rejoicing has sounded forth, there follows the discernment of spirits and the distribution of the gifts of the Spirit of which 1 Cor. 12:4 speaks. Christ says in John 7:38: 'He who believes in Me, out of his heart shall flow rivers of living water.' Waters denote the Holy Spirit, as in John 4:10. In the noonday heat spring water and rushing water are the most refreshing. The wells of salvation are the Gospel, sermons about Christ in various places, or even preachers of the Gospel. In that day, when waters will have flowed out to many because the Gospel has been preached, there will follow also in others the praise, that is, the sacrifice which you have."[2]

III. (Commenting on Gal. 1:15–16): "God set me apart from birth, called me by grace and revealed His Son to me. This sort of doctrine, which reveals the Son of God, is not taught, learned or judged by any human wisdom or by the

GOD IS FAITHFUL

Law itself; it is revealed by God first by the external word and then inwardly through the Spirit. Therefore the Gospel is a divine Word that came down from heaven and is revealed by the Holy Spirit who was sent for this very purpose. Yet this happens in such a way that the external Word must come first. For Paul himself did not have an inward revelation until he had heard the outward Word from heaven, namely, 'Saul, Saul, why do you persecute me?' (Acts 9:4). Thus he heard the external Word first, only then did he follow revelations, the knowledge of the Word, faith and the gifts of the Spirit."[3]

IV. "The Word they still shall let remain nor any thanks have for it. He's by our side upon the plain with his good gifts and Spirit."[4]

V. "I believe that by my own reason or strength I cannot believe in Jesus Christ, my Lord, or come to him. But the Holy Spirit has called me through the Gospel, enlightened me with his gifts, and sanctified and preserved me in true faith, just as he calls, gathers, enlightens and sanctifies the whole Christian church on earth and preserves it in union with Jesus Christ in the one true faith."[5]

VI. (From a sermon Luther preached on Mark 16:17–18 on Ascension Day, 1522): "If a Christian has the faith, he shall have power to do these signs....For a Christian has equal power with Christ, is one cake with Him....Where there is a Christian there is therefore the power to do such signs even now if it is necessary. But nobody should presume to exercise it if it is not necessary or required, for the apostles did not always exercise it either, only in order to proclaim the word of God and to confirm it by miracle."[6]

VII. (From a little treatise, "How to Pray"): "Frequently when I come to a certain part of 'Our Father' or to a petition, I land in such rich thought that I leave behind all set prayers. When such rich, good thoughts arrive, then one should leave the other commandments aside and offer room to those thoughts and listen in stillness and for all the world not put up obstructions. For then the Holy Spirit himself is preaching and one word of his sermon is better than a thousand of our prayers. I have also learned more from one such prayer than I would have received from much reading and writing."

"If the Holy Spirit would come in the course of such thoughts [methodical preparation for worshipfull prayer] and begins to preach in your heart with rich, illumined thoughts, do him the honor, let these rationally formulated thoughts, reflections and meditations fade away. Be still and listen for he knows better than you. And when he preaches note that and write it down. In this way you will experience miracles."[7]

VIII. Luther taught that the primary office (a special duty or position) is the ministry of the Word of God. However, he taught that that ministry is common to all Christians. All believers are "priests." "Paul confirms this in 1 Cor. 14:26 as he speaks not to the shorn or to a few, but to the whole church and each individual Christian: 'Each one of you has a hymn, a lesson, a revelation, a tongue or an interpretation.' And further on: 'For you can all prophesy one by one, so that all may learn and all be encouraged' (1 Cor. 14:31). For say, what is meant by 'each one of you?' and by 'all?' Can this mean only the shorn [the clergy]? These passages strongly corroborate that the ministry of the Word is the highest office in the church, that it is unique and belongs to all who are Christians, not only be right but by command."[8]

GOD IS FAITHFUL

NOTES

Chapter 2—I Met a Pharisee and He Was Me

1. *Webster's New World Dictionary* (Springfield, MA: Webster's, 1984), s.v. "Pharisee."

Chapter 3—The Reformation of a Lutheran Pharisee

1. David Dorpat, letter to the editor, *Advance*, March 1996, 35–36.

Chapter 6—John Chapter Six

1. Ewald M. Plass, *What Luther Says* (St. Louis: Concordia, 1959), 470.
2. Ibid., 470.
3. Ibid., 467.
4. Hugh Thomas Kerr, *A Compend of Luther's Theology* (Philadelphia: Westminster, 1945), 33.

Chapter 8—The Lutheran Church-Missouri Sin

1. Matthew 7:15–16; Galatians 1:6–9; Acts 19:8–10; 2 John 9–11; Romans 16:17–18; Titus 3:10; 2 Corinthians 6:14–18
2. *Formula for Concord Essays* (St. Louis: Concordia, 1971), 57.
3. "Theology of Fellowship" (paper presented at the Lutheran Conference—Missouri Synod Convention, New York, 1967), 28.
4. Ewald M. Plass, *What Luther Says* (St. Louis: Concordia, 1959), 470.

Chapter 11—A Touch of Heaven in Centerville

1. Theodore G. Tappert, *Book of Concord* (Philadelphia: Fortress Press, 1959), 42–45.

2. Ibid., 31.
3. Rufus Jones, as quoted by Charles P. Schmidt, *New Wine in New Wineskins* (Grand Rapids, MI: Fellowship of Believers, 1965), 4–5.

Chapter 13—There's Revelation and Then There's Revelation

1. Theodore G. Tappert, *Book of Concord* (Philadelphia, PA: Fortress Press, 1959), 312.
2. Ibid., 313.
3. Ibid., 313.
4. Ibid., 312.
5. Ibid., 441–442.
6. Ibid., 269.
7. Ibid., 275.
8. *Luther's Works, American Edition* (St. Louis: Concordia, 1955), 35.
9. Ibid., 130.
10. Bengt Hoffman, *Luther and the Mystics* (Minneapolis, MN: Augsburg, 1976), 188.
11. Emil Brunner, *The Christian Doctrine of God: Dogmatics* (London: Westminster John Knox Press, 1980).

Chapter 14—Prayer and the Means of Grace

1. Theodore G. Tappert, *Book of Concord* (Philadelphia, PA: Fortress Press, 1959), 313.
2. Ibid., 213.

Chapter 15—Let's Study the Bible

1. Alan Richardson, *A Theological Word Book of the Bible* (London: SCM Press, 1969).
2. "Theology of Fellowship" (paper presented at the Lutheran Conference—Missouri Synod Convention, New York, 1967), 29.
3. Gerhard Kittel, *Theologisches Worterbuch Zum Neuen Testament*, 6:851.
4. Ibid., 853.
5. Ibid., 854.
6. The Rev. Phil Gehlhar of DynaWorld Ministries, PO 10244, Westminster CA 92683, has researched and written extensively on the history of the Spirit's miraculous gifts, indicating that they have existed in the church every century up to today.

7. Letter from Rev. Santala to Dr. Qualben
8. *Spiritual Gifts* (Pueblo, CO: 1969)

Chapter 16—Let's Not Study the Bible

1. Taken from a tape of Dr. Danker's presentation, May 15, 1971.
2. Ibid.
3. Martin Franzmann, *Follow Me* (St. Louis: Concordia, 1961), 68–69.
4. *Webster's New Universal Unabridged Dictionary* (New York: Barnes & Noble, 1996), s.v., "charis."

Appendix III

1. Francis Pieper, *Christian Dogmatics* (St. Louis, MO: Concordia Publishing House, 1950), 289.
2. Merton Kelsey, *Tongues Speaking* (New York: Doubleday, 1964).

Appendix V

1. *Luther's Works*, CPH 40:36.
2. Ibid., 16:130
3. Ibid., AE 26, 73.
4. Martin Luther, *Ein Feste Burg*, "A Mighty Fortress Is Our God."
5. Martin Luther, *Luther's Small Catechism II*, 235.
6. *Luther's Works*, XI, 957:35.
7. Ibid., 43:193–211.
8. Ibid., AE 40:22–23.